PENGUIN BC

CASTE AS WC

Vrinda Nabar (b. 1948) studied at the universities of Bombay and Oxford. Her doctoral and post-doctoral work has dealt with post-colonial and women's issues and she has published widely in these areas. She has written regularly for Indian newspapers, and has presented programmes on radio and television. Her publications include *The Endless Female Hungers: A Study of Kamala Das* (New Delhi, 1994), *Snake-Skin and Other Poems of Indira Sant* (translated from the Marathi, Bombay, 1974), and *Post-Colonial Perspectives on the Raj and Its Literature* (Bombay, 1994) which she has co-edited. She is also represented in an anthology of poetry by Indian women poets edited by Pranab Bandopadhyay and in *In Their Own Voice: An Anthology of Contemporary Indian Women Poets*, edited by Arlene R.K. Zide (Penguin India, 1993).

Vrinda Nabar has been a Visiting Professor at Northwestern University (Evanston, USA) and the Open University (Milton Keynes, UK) and was, till recently, Chair of English at the University of Bombay. She is married to Sumit Bhaduri, has one daughter, Suranjana, and lives in Bombay.

Vrinda Nabar

Caste As Woman

PENGUIN BOOKS

Penguin Books India (P) Ltd., 210, Chiranjiv Tower, 43, Nehru Place, New Delhi 110 019, India
Penguin Books Ltd., 27 Wrights Lane, London W8 5TZ, UK
Penguin Books USA Inc., 375 Hudson Street, New York, NY 10014, USA
Penguin Books Australia Ltd., Ringwood, Victoria, Australia
Penguin Books Canada Ltd., 10 Alcorn Avenue, Suite 300, Toronto, Ontario M4V 3B2, Canada
Penguin Books (NZ) Ltd., 182-190 Wairau Road, Auckland 10, New Zealand

First published by Penguin Books India (P) Ltd. 1995

10 9 8 7 6 5 4

Typeset in Times Roman by Digital Technologies and Printing Solutions, New Delhi

Dedicated to
Sumit and Suranjana
who have always been there

Contents

Preface

This book has taken me nearly two years to write, but it was much longer gestating within me. At an intellectual, theoretical level, it is an attempt to analyse my sense of unease all through my growing years and, later, my time at university abroad, when feminist literature and the women's liberation movement were suddenly all around me.

At another, more fundamental, level this book is the culmination of innumerable experiences, personal and observed, as a woman in India, of responses, of moments of helpless rage and enormous gladness. It is born out of a long-felt need to contextualize all these different states of being in a disciplined manner. I had talked about them, agonized over them, read papers, published pieces in newspapers and journals, but had only vaguely considered that the search going on at the back of my mind could develop into an obsessive study.

It was David Davidar who first flung down the gauntlet. 'Write an Indian counterpart to *The Female Eunuch*,' he said over a half-hour coffee meeting! The more I thought about it, the more attractive his proposition seemed. It was challenging in a very basic way, because in spite of the growing literature on women's issues in India, the fact remained that we still lacked a text that had the compelling power to 'let the people think' (as Russell said in a very different context) in the manner *The Female Eunuch* had done.

Moreover, I wasn't even sure I wanted to merely produce an Indian *Female Eunuch*. Trying to do so would have negated my conviction that something different was needed. It was time we had a book on feminism in India which would interest average readers (the kind who would normally avoid anything with a vaguely feminist slant) because its terms of reference were close to their own. These, developed for the most part through language such as men do speak, called for a slightly divergent mode from the brilliant polemics of Greer's book.

David's faith in the ultimate soundness of my thesis encouraged me to move on from my first impassioned synopsis to a framework which best encompassed my study. Handicapped as I was by my lack of Sanskrit, I have had to rely heavily for my references on authorized translations and commentaries.

I realize that the pedant would see this as reason enough to dismiss this book outright. But the pedant would, in any case, not be sensitive to how my ignorance of Sanskrit itself proves a basic point in my argument, viz. that received ideas frequently acquire the status of unshakeable truths for the vast majority which, for various reasons, has no access to the original sources. This is all too clear in our socio-cultural practices and in our attitude to women.

While my use of sources may appear haphazard, there's method in my seeming madness. My purpose was not to attempt a comprehensive analysis—sociological or otherwise—of gender-operations in India. Personal experiences and observations form the nucleus of the book's *raison d'être*. These are contextualized as far as seemed possible, and necessary, in order to *understand* better the power of tradition and its hold on the Indian collective consciousness. I have argued in the book that tradition and individualism are two of the primary distinguishing features of the Indian and Western world-views, and that these differing outlooks would colour and contour any feminist agenda.

My references to various sources in the Indian sociocultural past reinforce my stand with respect to the hold tradition has over our present. These sources have seeped into the complex lives of cross-cultural factors and influenced the general overview of gender irrespective of differences in religion. Therefore, while my historical references are overwhelmingly 'Hindu', their contemporary relevance is pan-Indian in that they affect the general attitudes and prejudices confronting Indian women as a whole.

I am grateful to Professor Sindhu Dange of the Sanskrit Department at Bombay University for the untiring patience with which she guided me to various sources, and shared the fruits of her own research with me, though I must qualify this by adding that the conclusions drawn and the opinions expressed in this study are my own. They are largely independent of her scholarly but differing world-outlook, both in their stances and in the logic of their selectiveness.

Dr S. D. Karnik, Vice-Chancellor of Bombay University, recognized the importance and validity of my study and graciously allowed me to take off for a five-months' stay at Northwestern University, Evanston, USA. Mr R. M. Lala of the Sir Dorabji Tata Trust needed hardly any persuasion that my cause was worthy of a grant-in-aid. His generous gift helped me meet part of my horrendous travel expenses.

It was at Northwestern (1992) that I was able to complete a substantial part of my first draft. My research there helped develop a valuable comparative context for Indian and Western feminism, and made me aware of much crucial literature that our libraries could never have provided.

My time as Visiting Scholar in the English Department at Northwestern (kindly arranged by Professor Chris Herbert) made it possible for me to interact with several people engaged in research in the two areas which most concerned me: post-colonialism and women's studies. Of these I must make special mention of Professor Arlene Kaplan Daniels, Director of the Women's Studies Center, and Françoise Lionnet of the Department of French and Comparative Literature, both of whom enriched my stay through their warmth and professional interest in my work. Arlene made her vast library accessible to me and was herself a source of much useful information, while Françoise's own work in the area of post-colonial studies made our discussions particularly meaningful.

At a *personal* level, Evanston means a great deal to me, chiefly because of the many individuals who sustained my faith in myself—Ellie Harris, Virginia Rosenberg, Joyce Ibers, Neela Deshmukh and Ashok Kakkar being only a few of them. Though away from home, my siblings Vikram and Veena Nabar, through their many telephone calls and letters, kept alive the process of family caring and sharing which has always been so important to me.

I remember with affection and gratitude the zeal of colleagues and friends in India who so enthusiastically helped me with source-material of different kinds: Shireen Vakil, Nilufer Bharucha, S. Varalakshmi, and Nasreen Fazalbhoy. To my brother-in-law Suren Navlakha I owe many enlightening hours of rigorous scrutiny and unsparing argument, while Mary Bernard, Lygia Mathews and Roabin Mazumdar have given the word 'friendship' a wholly new dimension.

The three individuals who gave me my essential 'feminist' bearings are, alas, no longer alive: my parents Govind and Mira Nabar, and my maternal grandmother, K. Sundari Bhat. I can only inadequately acknowledge my debt to them, as to my husband Sumit Bhaduri who has kept his promise to 'tread softly' on my dreams, and has supported me through some of my worst crises. Finally, I hope that this book, when published, will help my daughter Suranjana to understand my priorities and obsessions a little better. For my part, her

'Oof, Ma, isn't your book finished *yet*?' was more of an incentive to push on than anything else could have been during the more difficult phases of my writing it!

Vrinda Nabar

Chapter 1

Our Women, Their Women

This book is being written at a time when the more extreme stances of feminism would appear to have played themselves out in the West, and the polemics of the militant feminism of the decades between 1960 and 1980 is being requestioned and redefined.

This is hardly surprising when one views it in the larger perspective of other fundamental changes that have occurred, changes whose repercussions are far too complex for any definitive analysis at this stage. I refer to the increasing disillusionment with socialist ideologies because, while feminist theory has not yet ostensibly incorporated these developments into its analytical mode, it would eventually have to review its course against their backdrop. For, perhaps inevitably, the feminist movement (especially in Europe) had identified itself increasingly with the framework of left-wing ideology. Now, however, the old structures of socialist thought have crashed down in a manner even its die-hard opponents could not have foreseen. Whatever Francis Fukoyama had had in mind when he first posited his 'end of history' argument, I do not think it had been this more or less total collapse of the very nucleus of the Cold War.

All these social and political changes would have to lead to crucial redefinitions in feminist theory, a realignment of goals and priorities among its more radical ideologues. If feminism has not yet taken cognisance of the implications of the collapse of socialist societies it will have to, if only to rework its theoretical allegiances. In fact, disillusionment with the New Left had manifested itself as early as 1970, when Robin Morgan published her essay 'Goodbye to All That' (included in *The Word of a Woman: Feminist Dispatches 1968–1992*, Norton), but it was a disillusionment that had more to do with personal experience (the relegation of women to making coffee, not policy) rather than with the actual theoretical framework of left ideology. There have been other rumblings within the movement almost since the very beginning of what can broadly be termed the growth of mainstream feminism in the 1960s.

It will not be my purpose in this book to summarize or review the literature of mainstream Western feminism in any detail, or to examine the validity of the term 'post-feminist' in the Western context. My primary concern here is with the Indian scenario. Such references as are made to the women's movement abroad would be ones which seem necessary to place the Indian situation in a larger, global context. This would highlight both our own differences from the theoretical premises of Western feminism, and the similarities which cut across cultural and societal boundaries.

Both aspects, again, seemed to me to be best illustrated by using American feminist literature as a primary (if not the only) cultural counterpoint: the increasing Americanization of the Third World—a swift and sure fate, if a superficial one, in the wake of satellite television and the ubiquitous nature of MTV—raises crucial questions about disparate contexts and the modalities which would best effect change.

A look at much of the literature of mainstream American feminism suggests that, contrary to the common perception of feminism as a monolithic construct, there has always been an ongoing battle among feminists about the road along which the journey was to be made, and the signposts that were to mark it. In some cases, differences arose when some of the cheer-leaders themselves acquired a modified perspective. Betty Friedan's *The Feminine Mystique* (W. W. Norton and Company Inc., New York, 1963) had been a crucial text which feminist thought in America had reacted to in various ways. Eighteen years later, Friedan's *The Second Stage* (Summit Books, New York, 1981) was reviled by many of her sisters as a betrayal of the feminist cause. Friedan's thesis in this book was based on her own perception of the inadequacies of the first feminist agenda. The movement, Friedan maintained, had reached the end of the road so far as its earlier insistence on the exclusive nature of the women's problem went: it was necessary to break through what had in turn become the *feminist* mystique (p. 27) and face the new reality of personal and political experience in order to move into the second stage.

The same year saw other crucial responses to two decades of American feminism. Among the most significant of these was *Ain't I A Woman*: *Black Women and Feminism* (South End Press, 1981) by black activist bell hooks. hooks questioned the simplistic equation the feminists had tried to cook up between the oppression of women and the oppression of blacks. She charged that by repeatedly treating women and blacks as analogous, feminists had clearly shown that to them the term 'woman' was synonymous with 'white women', the term 'blacks' with 'black men'. Therefore, hooks argued, feminism had its roots in a world-outlook coloured by racial imperialism. She pointed out that, throughout American history, such imperialism had misleadingly used the generic term 'women' even while referring exclusively to the experience of white women.

In *Feminist Theory: From Margin to Center* (South End Press, 1984), hooks argued once again for the essential difference between the black and white female experience, seeing it as a difference in perception of what the term 'oppressed' could mean to different social/ethnic/racial groups (p. 5 and p. 10).

The battle about feminism continues as variant literature projects its several areas of differences. One of the most volatile among recent publications is Susan Faludi's *Backlash: The Undeclared War Against American Women* (Crown Publishers, New York, 1991). Friedan had used the same term, i.e. backlash, in *The Second Stage* to describe the visible resurgence of hysterical hostility in all patriarchal societies to the progress made by women. Friedan's range of reference had, however, been far too general to be of more than passing cross-cultural interest, encompassing as it did parameters as disparate as America, Islam, and the Vatican! Faludi has used the term in a more culture-specific sense, to describe what she saw as a counter-assault on women's rights being perpetuated through all the organs of the American media. Such a counter-assault worked to hype the myth that the sexual revolution had meandered down a dead-end alley (pp. ix-xviii). Faludi questions the basis of the media thesis that women in the post-feminist era were miserable, alone, and shaky about feminism, or that they were not as committed as earlier to its ideals. She, like several others, questions the validity of the current national debate on the implications of feminism, seeing it as motivated and aimed at bull-dozing American women into reconsidering their status (synonymous to Faludi with convincing them that the fight is over and they've been the losers).

While the battle-lines are drawn, it is also clear from the discussions centred around terms like 'the mommy track' that post-feminism is widely perceived as a tangible socio-cultural experience. Research and national surveys would appear targeted towards showing that issues like marriage and motherhood are as obsessive as abortion and rape. According to a *Time* poll, fifty-one per cent of college students gave a stable, happy marriage and well-adjusted children more priority than the twenty-nine per cent who stressed career success (Nancy Gibbs, 'A Turning Point',

Span, May 1992, Vol. XXXIII Number 5, page 5). Even if one were, like Faludi, to see such surveys as calculated and statistically questionable, their very existence and scale suggests that the debate's post-feminist approach has a tangible if dubious rationale in the remaking of the American dream.

We in India are clearly a long way off from any base which would support the use of terms like 'post-feminist'. This is nowhere better illustrated than in the response of some sections of the Indian intelligentsia to the women's movement in India; a response conditioned, for the most part, by a vague understanding of reported disturbances in the feminist movement abroad. So inbred is the presence of what Fanon—in *The Wretched of the Earth* (Penguin, 1970)—had described as a bastard culture with a caricature audience that, in spite of the ongoing efforts of groups of women in India to Indianize the movement, the popular conception of the term feminism remains both ignorant and imitative.

Popular journals promote this ignorance by suggesting that the Indian woman has never had it so good. We are asked to believe that from testing the waters she has plunged in at the deep end. She storms male citadels, rewrites the home equations, and is on the threshold of a brave new sensual world ('Bahus, Betis and Businesses', *Femina*, 8 July 1992; 'The Changing Woman', *India Today*, 15 July 1992; 'Women on Top', *Femina*, 23 March 1994). There are people who would even summarily dismiss feminism as being over with. Popular response at a certain 'sophisticated' level is not unlike that of a Cambridge-educated (Indian) executive director of a British multinational company who maintained very authoritatively, over his second large Scotch in Bombay, that feminism was dated, 'played-out' to use his phrase. The answer to that, of course, is 'played-out' where?

As the literature referred to so far would indicate, it is doubtful whether the phrase would be valid even in the West, the backlash of the media counter-assault notwithstanding. Developments in black feminist theory, as well as more recent work by white feminists makes it evident that while feminist-related issues are being reconsidered, no one committed to feminism sees the battle as either won or insignificant.

Nearer home, even the more technologically-advanced and affluent nations like Japan clearly have a long way to go. I was an accidental eavesdropper some time back at a conversation-class in Evanston, Illinois. The place was a lounge outside the laundry-room in the basement of the apartment-block we were living in. As I waited for the dryer in the laundry to complete its cycle, I listened to a group of women from Korea, Taiwan and Japan trying to define existing social structures in their respective societies for their American teacher. What I overheard in terms of family structure, the male-female roles, the resentment against women (especially married women) working, discrimination at work, etc., sounded all too familiar, an echo of experiences both personal and observed in India.

My contention is that feminism hasn't even begun in any real sense in India. This is paradoxical because, on the one hand, there have been varying phases in what can broadly be termed the women's movement in India. In their book, *The Issues at Stake: Theory and Practice in the Contemporary Women's Movement in India* (New Delhi, Kali for Women, 1991), Nandita Gandhi and Nandita Shah outline the shifting goals and ideologies of the women's movement from the time it emerged as a part of the Social Reform Movement in the early nineteenth century to the present (pp. 16–23).

At the same time, as Gandhi and Shah also admit, the movement has been far too amorphous and rambling to have a meaningful impact except in a sporadic kind of way (pp. 23–5). Nor has the Indian Women's Movement evolved any clear-cut ideology or theory. It has not threatened the *status quo* in any significant way. There is no perceptible evidence that people see such a movement as *feminist*-related.

Feminism is a word most urban English-speaking Indians are familiar with, but their understanding of it remains foggy. There is a general scepticism about its usefulness. Conservative structures and ways of seeing have not so far allowed it to become a widely apprehended phenomenon. On the contrary, I watched my daughter and her friends perform a play written by a *female* schoolteacher of theirs, in which feminists were reduced to caricatures of domineering, housework-detesting women worthy of scorn. Awareness of feminism among the urban literate is largely confined to what is perceived of as the moral corruption of women abroad, a result of their unnatural freedom to think and choose what they want out of life! It is a fad which has something to do with not wearing a bra and unrestrained promiscuity. For most urban Indian males, feminism has continued to mean a bad word which, however, has tremendous comic-smutty potential. Since the Indian female has always been a considerably more conditioned product, usually coerced into a mindless acceptance of male *diktat,* the possibility of a reasoned, open-minded approach to the concept of feminism has been at best sporadic.

Yet, *feminism* and *feminist*, both late nineteenth century terms, were far removed from such interpretations. *Feminism* is reported as having originally meant the possession of female qualities, though it is now defined in the dictionary as a 'theory of the political, economic, and social equality of the sexes' (hooks, *Ain't . . .*, p. 194). *Feminist* was apparently first used in a book review in the *Athanoeum* of 27 April 1895, to denote a woman capable of fighting for and asserting her independence (Faludi: p. xxiii). The word is also found in Thomas Hardy's 'Preface' to the first edition of *Jude the Obscure* (April 1912). Hardy mentions a German reader who, in a letter to him, described the novel's controversial female protagonist, Sue Bridehead, as a woman of the feminist movement. She was the slender, pale bachelor girl, an intellectualized, emancipated bundle of nerves which modern conditions had been instrumental in producing (Macmillan, 1971, p. viii).

The ignorance about feminism in India is less surprising when one views it in the context of experiences like the one narrated by Elizabeth Fox-Genovese (*Feminism without Illusions: A Critique of Individualism;* The University of North Carolina Press, Chapel Hill and London, 1991) about an undergraduate student who progressed from a view of feminism as implying lesbianism, bra-burnings, men-hating and aggressiveness (p. 1) to a position where she considered herself a proponent of feminism (p. 3). Both reflect a basic ignorance about feminist issues, backed by media-distortion and older forms of patriarchal resistance.

One of the reasons for the sustained misapprehension about feminism among the Indian intelligentsia may be the failure of committed feminists in this country to provide a text that would both arouse public attention and be taken seriously, a text that would be of interest to a significant cross-section of readers, young and old, male and female, given the fact that this readership would still remain a somewhat limited one in proportion to India's population, and that the audience for literature in India is, anyway, limited.

As long as such a text—which addresses itself in words such as men do use to issues which are primarily Indian remains unwritten, more than half of India's population remains faceless and undefined except in traditional, androcentric terms. Several invaluable studies of women-related issues, both in the form of recent articles and books, have remained inaccessible or of little interest except to scholars, researchers, and those with a motivated interest in women's studies. In a society still largely suspicious of changes in the lifestyle of its women, obviously erudite studies which function within a remote (because unfamiliar) framework, can end up having only a marginal impact.

The main obstacle in writing a book that seeks to arouse popular interest would be the impossibility of a comprehensive female representation. My argument, in spite of my best efforts, would be substantially limited by my urban, middle-class background. The intellectual rationale for the argument would in turn be conditioned by my own position within the urban set-up, however hard I may try to decondition my responses. The boundaries of caste, class and economic disparity may seem to call for a book in themselves. But it is hoped that the categories which apply to the Indian woman and the framework within which she is placed are, at one level, all-encompassing. It is perhaps possible to address areas of experience and manifestations of social mores which can be broadly classified as being of immediate relevance to the Indian female and her way of life. It is these that I hope to at least partly examine and critically scrutinize.

The paradox I referred to in the Indian Women's Movement operates in several deceptive ways. In the early Seventies, when the feminist movement was in its most militant form, several of my female acquaintances in England used to express the view that Indian women had received a major shot in the arm because their Prime Minister was a woman. What these women apparently did not see was that while India may have seemed to lead the way in a manner of speaking (Golda Meir and Margaret Thatcher followed on Mrs Gandhi, though Mrs Bandaranaike of Sri Lanka had preceded her), this fact meant very little in terms of the Indian female reality. It may be seen as reflecting a fundamental misconception about the abiding role of the individual seen as representative of a process of social change—the individual as history, so to say. I am not casting aspersions on Mrs Gandhi's value as a symbol to Indian women at all levels, or on the sincerity of her commitment or its achievement in national terms. My own reservations about Mrs Gandhi have very little to do with my argument that her being Prime Minister signified very little about the Indian Woman and had a great deal to do with her class, family, and her location in Indian political history.[1]

Similarly, while individual women may have made it to the top in several spheres today, the bahus, betis and their businesses can hardly be seen as reflecting a meaningful general shift. Even the articles which exalt such 'breakthroughs' are aware of the deception, and define their parameters in questionable ways. The *India Today* piece mentioned earlier admits that its coverage is of the middle-class, educated urban woman, but its rationalization of this limited representation has itself become a primary dividing issue on the assumptions of feminism in the West. According to *India Today*, it has looked at only the middle class woman because the rural woman has always worked any way (p. 55).

Such a defence can only reveal the limited world-view of its proponents, for it ignores the socio-cultural reality of work as a double-edged symbol: of freedom, or the lack of it. For instance, according to bell hooks, for the black woman who had always done 'man's work' anyway, labouring in the fields and on the large plantation-homes, the leisured life-style of the white lady of the house symbolized freedom from oppression. This may well be the way the rural woman, about whom *India Today* generalizes, also views the value of work. The question for these women would not be whether one can choose to work but whether one can choose not to. The women employed as 'household domestics' or *bais* are equally oppressed by their absence of choices. To them, work is not liberating but a daily reminder of their economic and class oppression.

Even among the middle class, the general trend is far less spectacular. This would of course be true of all societies, and Friedan in *The Feminine Mystique* had shown how seductive and all-pervasive the idea of domesticity and gentle companionship could be. The ethos of Friedan's Fifties evokes images of the present-day middle-class syndrome in India, but it also permeates every strata of our society, since its message is that women have a feminine role in which they are happiest.

Popular American literature of the period reflected Friedan's 'mystique'. It may be witnessed in the innumerable silent, frustrated, deeply unhappy women of a Raymond Chandler or Ross MacDonald novel, wives of successful men attempting to cope with what Friedan called the 'problem without a name'. Friedan's portrayal of the millions of American women who modelled themselves on pictures of pretty suburban housewives (p. 18) is also found in Ira Levin's popular novel *The Stepford Wives*, in which the theme of happy domesticity is imaginatively used to give it a sinister dimension.

In this horror fantasy, the Stepford males collude in a game which is well-devised and concealed, but which aims at a transformation of their little social world into a fiendish Utopia. The Stepford women as we see them have a compulsive need to clean, scrub, wax and polish. To a young woman who has recently moved into Stepford, they seem almost robot-like, uniformly impeccable, unruffled, with well-proportioned bodies.

However, when she accidentally discovers that they had once been articulate women, involved in various women's issues, she probes deeper and begins to suspect that these women are indeed robots, cleverly modelled on the less submissive wives who have been murdered. Her attempts to resist the same fate prove futile when her own feminist husband joins the male conspiracy. The novel ends with the Stepford community more or less converted into an exemplary, happy suburb—the American dream embodied in this glorification of the feminine mystique syndrome.

Not the greatest of novels, certainly, but interesting because of the way in which a perceived social ambience is creatively, if satirically, used to highlight its sinister possibilities. The hysteria of Faludi's thesis, written so many years later, suggests that a motivated campaign to eliminate women who step out of the accepted line of social conformism is both conceivable and in operation.

However, since I referred to the presence of the feminine mystique among innumerable middle-class Indian women, the specific manifestations of this mystique may be briefly examined by referring to literature with a mass-appeal. In the popular women's journal *Femina* (23 July 1992), a successful actress feels obliged to tell her readers that though an actress by choice and a teacher by profession, she is a housewife by preference! The article reasserts the desirability of this 'preference', by insisting that it is this ordinary desire to cook for her family and spend time with them on every holiday that makes this 'extraordinary' actress such a 'unique and special individual' (p. 65).

It may be safely claimed that, whatever the class-background, the general trend in India is one where ordinariness implies status quo, where women are brainwashed into imagining that their position as housewives makes them better women and individuals who preserve the sanity of the nation. Among the middle class, however, there is an unfortunate degree of sanctimoniousness in both the stay-at-homes who, convinced of their do-good roles are critical of the career women, and some of the career women who, in the process of establishing an identity, have acquired a brashness which antagonizes even those who may be sympathetic towards the emancipation of women.

Such antagonism, coupled with basic patriarchal resistance to not so much the idea but the implications of change could result in a glorification of the older generation prototype, the stay-at-home grandmother figure. This resistance falsifies the larger reality by emphasizing only its softer aspects. Such is Makarand Paranjape's 'The New Woman is a Selfish Woman' (*Femina*, 8 October 1992) which contrasts two generations of Indian women. One of these is already a great-grandmother, and Paranjape describes her in glowing terms. She is at work, chopping vegetables on the old-fashioned vili. Though bent with age, she is still an energetic worker. Her free time is filled with innumerable diversions—she makes wicks for the lamps placed in front of the gods, or dolls, handkerchiefs, sweaters; she embroiders, mends torn clothes, is never idle.

In contrast, we have her great-granddaughter, home from school: T-shirt and cut-offs, Walkman and earphones, spiky hair-do. She is dressed to the hilt for a party she is off to. Paranjape's comparison of the two leads him to conclude, depressingly, that the new woman doesn't know how to give, only to take, and with a vengeance.

These are damning statements of an extreme kind. They will be taken up for detailed analysis later on, when the dilemmas of contemporary Indian women are discussed. The fundamental confusion in which they are embedded may however be illustrated in the get-up of a more recent issue of *Femina* (23 March 1994), where the lead feature, 'Women on Top', rubs shoulders with 'Manly Acts'. The first of these exalts the new woman who has hit the highs in management, while the second applauds women for spending 'the best part of their lives pandering to . . . [manly] whims to enable them to continue with their manly acts'. These include a choice of several roles—'her own little girl act, weak woman act or motherly act'.

The recent upsurge of fundamentalism in turn raises fears about the future of Indian feminism, such as it is. It has been regrettably seen that any form of fundamentalism is essentially hostile to women. Abroad, many white women who had grown up in the shadow of men like Malcolm X had come, eventually, to fear the anti-woman stance of their fundamentalist approach. Even before *their* disillusionment, black feminists had berated their black male leaders for their support of patriarchy (hooks, *Ain't* . . . , p. 94–5). In doing so, they had accused white feminists of a bourgeois avant-gardeism which failed to acknowledge that their dominant values projected, in a merely inverted form, a white supremacist class-structure which had its roots in capitalist patriarchy (hooks, *Margin* . . ., p. 5, 18). It seems, therefore, that the implications of fundamentalism in the feminist context were close enough home even in the West. This should only serve to accentuate the threat of fundamentalist forces to the Indian woman, since her position has been defined, more or less consistently, by fundamentalist attitudes of conventional orthodoxy.

Certain other factors (besides the more basic differences of cultural history and tradition and their relationship to the way in which Indian society perceives its women) may perhaps pinpoint specific social needs and solutions. In *The Female Eunuch,* Germaine Greer had questioned the focus of, for example, Betty Friedan's National Organization of Women, and of women politicians who saw female interests as implying the interests of women as dependants who need protection from things like easy divorce and Casanova exploitations. The feminist agenda, however, has made it clear that such scepticism cannot come in the way of the politicization of the movement. This is unfortunately even more imperative in a set-up like ours where the exploitation of large numbers of women from all classes of society is condoned in spite of laws to the contrary. Our Manjushree Sardas[2] and Tarvinder Kaurs[3] continue to be murdered for dowry in spite of the fact that dowry is illegal; the Shahbano[4] case rocked the boat of a Central government, but has had little effect on the abuse of personal law; a Roop Kanwar[5] can be exalted to near-sainthood a century after the practice of sati was officially banned.

Moreover, over the past few decades we have witnessed a large-scale degeneration of all the institutionalized forms of societal working. This has infected nearly all areas of operation in India, creating conditions of a near breakdown of the system. A degree of institutionalization, even politicization, therefore seems desirable if only as a life-line. As Gandhi and Shah have pointed out (pp. 22–23), in spite of the criticism of the women's movement (its leadership is predominantly middle class; it lacks a theory and a strategy for seeking State power) it has contributed to several notable achievements. It has chosen to pressurize the State rather than function as a political opposition party and seize power. In this way, it has worked towards State awareness of forms of female exploitation and their redressal through official policy.

It is against this background that one needs to examine the question raised by Heera Nawaz, viz. 'Will the National Commission For Women Work?' (*Femina*, 8 July 1992). Nawaz admits that there may be justifiable scepticism about the success of this commission, given the track record of other national commissions. However, our context is that of a society which has more than 400 million women, of whom the majority are poverty-stricken and illiterate. Nawaz lists *some* of their problems—unemployment, wage discrimination, molestation, rape, deprivation of property, exploitation, harassment in hostels, incessant dowry demands, etc.

These are global issues, with this basic caveat. The disparate contexts of the Western world and ours arise from the essential difference between an affluent society incorporating levels of poverty and a fundamentally deprived society with levels of affluence which have left other processes of social evolution severely alone. I refer to a society in which a chief justice of the Supreme Court, speaking in his official capacity, makes a series of retrograde statements about the function and role of Indian women and then retracts in the face of feminist anger and wrath, but maintains in doing so that this was his personal opinion and he did not mean to hurt the sentiments of any group of women! The furore that erupted over the attempt to introduce a uniform civil code after the Shahbano incident made it clear that the fundamentalist support of the personal law is really an assertion of the power of that law to control both the community and its patriarchal core (Gandhi and Shah, p. 255).

In such a context it seems more than ever necessary that the recognition of women's problems be made part of official policy, particularly given the connection in India between politics (i.e. official power) and organization (including labour-unions). In the article I have just referred to, Nawaz warns that the largely 'recommendatory' status of the commission may prevent any radical, change-inducing moves. The commission will remain relatively ineffectual unless given the power to translate its perceptions into action-oriented programmes and to enforce these. For this to happen, a total dependence on government funds would be undesirable. The commission should be free to tap private sources, involve itself with voluntary organizations and recognize the need for grassroot involvement. Nawaz argues for the importance of consciousness-raising and state-level commissions which would investigate regional problems.

Consciousness-raising in fact remains a crucial need, first because of the very nature of any women's struggle (not *us* against *them*, i.e. men, but *us* with *them*), and second because of the obstinate paradox in Indian society of radicalism combined with orthodoxy in a long historical tradition. This paradox is compounded because of the shifts in attitudes through different ages on the one hand and their repeated misinterpretation in the popular consciousness on the other. Given the colonial context of our recent past such misinterpretation, usually at the hands of demagogues who have little real knowledge of the past, has glorified the so-called 'native' customs and traditions, seeing feminism as superfluous in a society where women are allegedly deified and respected. Various sources, arbitrarily and selectively chosen, have been used to suggest that Indian women do not need a corrupting militancy which is the product of an alien culture.

The confused acceptance of such arguments by most Indians has a great deal to do with the fact that there is, indeed, historic evidence that our women once enjoyed a social status perhaps unparalleled in human history. Yasca's *Nirukta* makes references to such a status in the pre-epic period, difficult to imagine today, given our track-record in this area ever since. It is tempting, under the influence of post-colonial nationalism, to ignore that what may broadly be termed the 'Indian' consciousness *today* is clearly the product of a very different world-view as regards women. The legacy of the dharma-śāstras, with their anti-women thrust, has proved extraordinarily powerful in post-epic times and has continued to shape popular belief about the nature and role of women.

The Jaṇābāīs,[6] Mirābāīs[7] and Bahiṇābāīs[8] in our literature are isolated female voices who affirm the paradox of a radical defiance superimposed upon the prevalent conservatism. They should be viewed as victims who dared to speak out, and whose writing contains a feminist consciousness in embryo. Their poetry exhibits specific problems associated with being Hindu women from very diverse backgrounds. Jaṇābāī describes the double injustice of being a woman and a Śūdra. As a Śūdra, her caste was doomed to exclusion from any knowledge of the scriptures, which privilege was denied all women any way. Mirābāī was married into a princely family but rebelled against its constraints and became a devotee of Kṛṣṇa. Bahiṇābāī, a Brahmin, transgressed both in choosing the low-caste Tukārām as her mentor and in becoming better-known than her Brahmin husband!

While all three women are among the principal saint-poets in the Indian bhakti tradition, their themes have a great deal to do with the oppressiveness of religio-social mores, especially in relation to women. In all three, the concept of female brazenness, seen in social terms, is inseparable from the stances adopted. While Jaṇābāī and

Mirābāī glory in their alleged loss of modesty, Bahiṇābāī refers to her husband's sense of shame at her unconventionality and vows, through lines which are an ironic reaffirmation of Manu's code for good wives, to experience intellectual freedom and salvation through serving him.

It is erroneous to interpret such examples of female outspokenness as the rule and overlook the troubling signifiers embedded in them which suggest otherwise. Such woman-specific distortions are especially disturbing when coupled with attempts at the wrong kind of consciousness-raising of fundamentalists of different religious convictions because, apart from the insanity unleashed, such fundamentalism, as already argued, is ultimately hostile to the interests of women.

It is perhaps in recognition of the special needs of the Indian social structure that the Indian Women's Movement has been composed of various support groups which work towards asserting the woman's membership in a community. These endeavours have permeated to the grassroots level. One of the most significant among recent examples of this is that of the 'saathins' in rural Rajasthan (Harinder Baweja, 'The Second Sex Awakens', *India Today*, 31 October 1992). In a culture where segregation of the sexes is the normal code of prescribed behaviour, such female bonding is natural and not necessarily directed towards any form of social change. It can, however, be exploited to implement such change, though the extent to which this can be successfully done is limited.

A question I was asked quite often while this book was being written was what I meant by *feminism in the Indian context.* The reservations I sensed in this question seemed to be more against the implied nativism of such feminism. To many Western white women, bell hooks notwithstanding, feminism is so global in its relevance, its terms of reference, the areas of struggle it defines, and its agenda for reform, that the idea of these as being less relevant to another cultural context seems difficult to understand.

Yet in another, literary, context, critic John Oliver Perry has convincingly argued against using 'Eng. Lit.' criteria for Indian English poetry merely because it is written in a language derived from Amero-British culture. Perry recognizes the unsuitability of an arbitrary application of the essential values of a European-based culture to one which is entirely different and composed, in turn, of various and mixed cultural value systems (*Absent Authority: Issues in Contemporary Indian English Criticism,* Sterling Publishers, New Delhi, 1992, p. 29).

Perry's thesis may be appropriately extended to the parameters of the feminist question. Since I have earlier referred to popular Indian magazines on the grounds that these best image the present-day consciousness of a society, a reference to an article from the January 1993 issue of *Today's Chicago Woman* may perhaps help. The writer is Grace Kaminkowitz, a public affairs consultant, and panelist on a radio programme called *Inside Politics*.

Reviewing her '1993 Wish List', Kaminkowitz says she would like women's top priorities to receive attention. Kaminkowitz groups these broadly under the following heads: guaranteed health care; equal pay; discrimination laws; help for parents along with expanded, affordable and accessible quality child care; a family and medical leave act; prevention of violence against women; increased funding for women's education; an increase in the minimum wage; funds for job training; increased tax credit for child care; new or expanded after-school programmes for children; full abortion rights; tax credit for homemakers (a category widely prevalent in India), and more child support.

Those who are sceptical about culture-specific feminism would argue that these are what most women need, would want—a stand acceptable if one assumes a certain level of informed thinking on the subject. After all, the list does indicate common areas of struggle against various forms of female exploitation. However, the answer as to what makes the Indian situation different has a great deal to do with different world-orders, in turn derived from differing cultural traditions and the codes these evolve over a period of time. One of the principal areas of focus in my study has to do with the role of tradition in our social existence and the need for feminism to first discredit some of the legacies of this tradition. This would in turn historicize the subject. This is not unlike the methodology of some of the seminal literature of Western feminism, wherein the revolt was directed against the constraining influence of Judaeo-Christian prejudices and their effect on the collective unconscious of societies where they prevailed.

Something of the way in which a questioning mind can seek to liberate a faith from its shackling prejudices, by insisting on their contemporaneous as against absolute relevance, may be seen in a fairly recent publication by the controversial Episcopal Bishop of Newark, John Shelby Spong (*Born of a Woman: A Bishop Rethinks the Birth of Jesus,* Harper, San Francisco, 1992).

The book's main strength is its writer's conviction that if faith is to be meaningful, it must address its age and be as revolutionary in each age as it was when it first came into being. It is only an understanding of this dynamic principle underlying a faith (and this incorporates change) which can liberate its believers. Ostensibly motivated by the Bishop's experience of how the invisible walls of dogma imprisoned his own daughters, the book considers that most central symbol, the Immaculate Conception, as a myth born in a specific age. Its author sees the tradition born of this myth as having oppressed women and done them enormous harm. He recognizes the need for fundamentalists to throw open their windows to the winds of change if they wish Christianity to survive as a potent force in the twenty-first century. According to him, this can only happen if the negative female image centering on the figure of the Virgin is destroyed.

There is every reason to maintain that except among the orthodox believers in the West, the old traditional view born of Judaeo-Christian myths does not have a particularly strong hold. However, one is still aware of its unconscious influence on the popular psyche. There is an area somewhere between orthodox faith and scepticism where one's mental make-up has its popular being. Those who are in revolt, or not practising believers, ultimately relate to a given tradition: all their terms of reference are to it. They are influenced by its basic premises even while they may reject its more obtrusive, strident manifestations. In other words, it is not difficult for the Western view to be placed within its religio-cultural heritage. This is true whether one goes as far back as Saint Theresa or Joan of Arc, or looks at the evolution of feminist ideology in the twentieth century. Fox-Genovese traces the contemporary model of sisterhood to the fundamentalist assumption that womanhood is a universal condition. This assumption, she points out, contradicts the reality of different women's lives, and ignores the fact that contemporary American feminism arose and developed within specific historical conditions (p. 17). An example is the way in which, in a very brief span of time during the Enlightenment, the period of the new rationalism in the eighteenth century, women who had long been viewed as evil began to be depicted as essentially good—a process which incorporated and consolidated the ultimate vision of motherhood as woman's highest mission (p. 124).

In a similar way, the tradition most Indian women would relate to is the Hindu one. In fact, the extent to which this relationship moulds popular ideology is far more visible, given the manner in which feudal inequalities still control the operations of power in India. And while there are other religious communities within the Indian subcontinent, each in turn has been influenced historically and culturally by the other. The strictures regarding codes of behaviour and forms of social purdah are found in both Hinduism and Islam, and similar patterns may be observed in the other minority groups: Sikhs, Parsis, Christians, Jews, Buddhists and Jains. There is a certain image conjured up by the nomenclature Bhāratīya nārī,[9] which cuts across religious boundaries, and which women by and large conform to or question in varying degrees of defiance and revolt.

The importance of the hold of tradition and mythology on the Indian subconscious should not be undermined. In very crucial ways it affects sensibility responses to an extent not experienced in the West. Very few men or women in the West, even among the more conservative believers, would *consciously* use the Virgin Mary to uphold present-day ideals of female perfection or purity. On the other hand, the readiness with which most Indians grasp at mythological stereotypes like Sītā[10] or Sāvitrī,[11] or their reservations about Draupadī,[12] are an obvious indication that, for us, time future is indeed contained in time past.

There may be several reasons for this. Unlike the Western, linear view of history, the Indian has tended to perceive history as a flowing together of layers of past and present. The Western view sees past, present and future as causally linked, but to the Indian the past has a living presence which serves contemporary needs. While the nationalist upsurge may have given the past a more urgent and specific role, it had never ceased to structure the Indian consciousness through the ages. This may have something to do with a world-outlook which is sentimental, even emotionalistic and melodramatic, rather than pragmatic and utilitarian. At any rate, the average Indian simply *accepts* the validity of the past without questioning too deeply, or threateningly, its sociocultural rationale or the desirability of viewing it as a universal absolute.

We are fond, in India, of speaking of an ideal past when women were equal with men and no discrimination was visible. Such an unreal vision ignores the Sītās and Draupadīs who are as much the postscripts of that allegedly idyllic age as are the male protagonists of our national epics. The myth denuded would reveal a pattern of unequal prescription. Sītā does not merely follow Rāma into the forest, but has to prove her chastity after being rescued from Rāvaṇa who had abducted her. Draupadī is pawned in a game of dice, a clear indication of her status as a dispensable commodity owned by the five Pāṇḍava brothers to whom she is married. Both Sītā and Draupadī herald an ongoing tradition of long-suffering women whose real heroism is overlaid with the message of devotion and service to their husbands, a glorification of these qualities so that martyrdom is seen, in some cases, as preferable, desirable, virtuous, and even imperative.

In various parts of this book, I have attempted to specify how these stereotypes affect our creative impetus. At this stage, I need only point out that our refusal to subject these images to the process of social change, our ingrowing pride in them, makes the woman question somewhat different from the way the West understands it. At the same time, in spite of the somewhat submerged presence of myth in the Western outlook, its detrimental influence must operate substantially, enough for someone like the Bishop of Newark to speak out on the dangers of not confronting and altering it. The imperatives for a hard look at *our* own tradition of anti-woman sentiment are even more compelling, for it is only by doing so that one can not merely agitate for, but hope to effect, change.

This is, however, more easily said than done because it involves a drastic overhaul of a consciousness rooted in another perspective. Something of our all-embracing blindness in this respect may be seen in the fact that even today the Shankaracharya of Puri objects to a woman reciting the Vedas; the principal of a college in Calcutta attempts to dictate a code of dress for *female* pupils; a woman obstetrician justifies gender infanticide on sociocultural-humanitarian grounds (see Chapter 2); a menstruating woman is forbidden participation in any religious ritual even among the urban élite, and so on.

Feminism in the West had its hour of glory in the Seventies. By the time the Eighties arrived, the dogmatic militancy had been tempered with a degree of willingness to look at women-related issues in a wider context. It was seen that extreme stances could ignore the larger reality in terms of the pressures, instinctual and conditioned, that the emancipation of women could pose.

The literature of feminism reflects these shifts. As Faludi points out in her comprehensive if brief summary (pp. 320–1), Greer's *The Female Eunuch* (1970) gave way to *Sex and Destiny* (1984); Susan Brownmiller's *Against Our Will* (a landmark work on rape which appeared in 1975) was followed, eleven years later, by *Femininity* (1986). Even Erica Jong, Faludi reminds us, recanted in *Ms.* magazine. By the end of the decade, Jong's 'saucy' Isadora Wing (*Fear of Flying*) had been replaced by the embittered protagonist in *Any Woman's Blues,* a book that rejected the sexual revolution and projected the despair of so-called liberated women (p. xi). More recently, Camille Paglia who calls herself a feminist has published two books of which the first, *Sexual Personae*, is already a best-seller. This has been followed by *Sex, Art and American Culture* (1992). In both she appears to propagate age-old myths about issues like pornography and, more specifically, rape.

Some of the contradictions inherent in hard-line feminism had been perceived by earlier feminists. Sheila Rowbotham had pointed out the essential difference between sex and class, i.e. between the oppression of women and the oppression of other groups (*Woman's Consciousness, Man's World,* Pelican, 1973, p. 117). Following her experience as a reporter assigned to do a piece on Playboy Bunnies, Gloria Steinem had provocatively alleged that *all* women were bunnies. In the Eighties, black feminists like bell hooks insisted that the white feminist perception of oppression and patriarchy was a privileged one that ignored fundamental factors like race and colour.

The Second Stage explored some of the contradictions and insisted that these could not be dismissed through mere rhetoric. These contradictions include emancipation and relationships with men; marriage and the male-female equation; family and professional needs; professionalism and domesticity; the break-up of relationships/marriages; etc.

Given the media-boom in the Seventies and Eighties, the feminist wave in the West received immediate and widespread exposure in India. Its persuasive rhetoric wooed a large number of articulate women engaged in trying to break through the conventions of a hidebound, traditionally patriarchal society. The earliest attempts to draw in women on a global scale through various internationally organized seminars and conferences, along with the growing availability of feminist literature, in turn led to several notable attempts to focus on real issues: the setting up of a journal like *Manushi*, a publishing venture like Kali for Women which has promoted some extremely significant literature on Indian women and women-related subjects, activist groups like the Forum Against Rape (which changed its name to Forum Against Oppression of Women) and so on.

Other political events within India may have contributed to the organized struggles against forms of social violence, including violence against women. Gandhi and Shah trace the beginnings of the present campaign against violence to the post-Emergency period (p. 36). The Emergency, which was in effect from 1975 to 1977, certainly shook the middle class out of its complacency by jeopardizing the civil liberties *it* had always taken for granted in post-Independence India. Some of the issues activists addressed themselves to as a result of this new consciousness were rape, dowry deaths (both murders and suicides), sexual harassment including 'eve-teasing', and so on.

But if the movement abroad had begun to manifest a

revolt within its ranks along with the social counter-resistance which Faludi terms a 'backlash', the movement in India, such as it is, has been embedded in these contradictions from the very start. Those who subscribe to left of centre ideologies have even dismissed the resolution of women's issues to the post-revolutionary period, seeing class struggle as the main issue which is being diluted by feminist irrelevancies such as the oppression of women (*A Space Within the Struggle : Women's Participation in People's Movements,* ed. Ilina Sen, Kali for Women, 1990, pp. 2–3).

This is qualitatively similar to the arguments of black militant male leaders who emphasized the struggle against white supremacist oppression as the primary struggle, a stance which has been questioned and criticized by black feminists. hooks, for example, charges them with righteously supporting black patriarchy as if it were a positive reaction against racist values (*Ain't* . . ., pp. 94–5).

There has been no organized radical revolt which has had any significant impact on the way a large section of Indian society looks at the problem. As late as 1985, the Bharatiya Janata Party's women's wing in Pune demonstrated against women's liberationist groups, claiming that most women were happy being mothers and wives and did not consider themselves oppressed. More important, this view was expressed by Mrs Pramila Dandavate, a political activist associated with militant, socialist views (Gandhi and Shah, p. 24).

Such resistance at its most basic level refuses to recognize that problems exist and are significant enough to require a planned agenda. Moreover, while contradictions may be found in virtually all movements and while, as already seen, the women's movement abroad has had to counter these in its varied phases, the vastly different scenario in India encompasses contradictions of a kind undreamed-of in mainstream (Western) feminist philosophy. Factors such as caste, class, economic deprivation, sectarian fragmentedness, size and numbers, overpopulation, the growing power of fundamentalist forces, the sway of superstition, female foeticide, and above all the essential nature of what is broadly termed Hinduism combine to create a situation which defies any easy solution.

It is for this reason that, even among the literate middle class, ignorance about the basic issues of the women's movement vitiates its more positive advances. Nirad C. Chaudhuri's analysis of the Hindu view of life could perhaps best explain why this is so: According to Chaudhuri, Hinduism emphasized the force of 'collective faith' and exacted 'public obedience' from its followers. As a result, private or individual acts of defiance had no significance in its broad scheme of things (*Hinduism,* OUP, 1979, p. 121). To the vast majority of the middle class, *Manushi*, Kali for Women, or the Forum Against the Oppression of Women remain at best peripheral details.

If one looks at the media coverage of the feminist movement from the Sixties onwards, it becomes clear that a principal reason why most Indians (men and women) have remained sceptical about feminism is because the kind of events publicized in India wore a bizarre streak that was totally out of sync with the language people spoke. To start with, it was 'Women's Lib.' rather than 'feminism' which most people heard of. Gloria Steinem has commented on the trivializing potential of terms like 'Women's Lib.' or Women's Libber', pointing out that no one would dream of using terms like 'Algerian Lib.' or 'Black Libber' ('Words and Change', in *Outrageous Acts and Everyday Rebellions,* Holt, Rinehart and Winston, New York, 1983, p. 155).

The phrase 'Women's Lib.' had a dilettantish flavour to a culture that had learned not to oppose but encourage institutions like Mahila Mandals, non-threatening organizations which promoted female solidarity in a conventional framework not unlike that of traditional Women's Guilds in the West: fêtes, cookery competitions, recipe contests, harmless talks, etc. And when newspapers reported events like the infamous bra-burning incident (which never took place), this only strengthened the conviction that 'Women's Lib.' was another aberration in the world of Western trends, like topless swimsuits and see-through shirts, mini-skirts, and the 'promiscuous' hippies.

This response was consolidated by other happenings in the Sixties and early Seventies. India suddenly became the Mecca of hordes of Westerners seeking 'spiritual peace' on beaches, in ashrams, through yoga, meditation and hash. In a sense, India was an easy option for these dharma bums (to borrow Jack Kerouac's colourful phrase), because of its socio-economic structure, its easy acceptance of a 'catching-flies' lifestyle (inevitable, given the large-scale unemployment and poverty), and the sloppiness in dress extending to degrees of nudity (again inevitable in a poor country). There was another factor—the Indian reverence for the white sahib, and the consequent tolerance of forms of freakish behaviour as a sahib prerogative, born out of two hundred odd years of a colonized existence.

But there was one factor which Indians were unprepared for. While sloppy, hirsute males were easily ignored, what erupted before them suddenly was large-scale sexual 'promiscuity': men and women copulating on the beaches, being sexually demonstrative in public, pairing off with one another in a clearly non-marital relationship. This was a time when women's magazines had not quite got past the stage of coyly referring to sexual activity in terms of 'marital relations'. The Western woman was an eye-opener, for male promiscuity was nothing new in this ancient land. Her modes of dress and behaviour were seen as deliberately provocative. They marked her out as the bra-burning female prototype of the 'Women's Lib.' movement.

I remember the reaction in a middle-class residential colony in Pune in the early Seventies when a German male resident on deputation to an Indian company had a young

Swedish woman from the nearby Rajneesh ashram not only move in with him but move out a day before his wife flew out to join him. There was no outrage as regards his peccadilloes, but the woman was commonly referred to as 'that Rambha'[13] and provided considerable amusement, the men digging each other in the ribs after each smutty innuendo while their wives giggled in implicit acceptance of *their* own contrasting sobriety and fidelity.

This incident is reasonably representative of how the middle class by and large perceived the new sexuality which was only one of the issues of the women's movement. Events like the International Women's Year were occasions for an endless stream of puerile humour. In Bombay, a Rotarian President received thunderous applause at a panel-discussion when he said that, it being the International Women's Year, he had had to seek his wife's permission before he could speak.

Since the vote had come so naturally with the transfer of power and the establishment of a democratic India, even the suffragette struggle did not signify very much. The image of the suffragettes was not helped, either, by their general depiction in literature and the cinema as earnest but drab women. The struggle for Indian Independence had thrown up a sufficiently large number of female militants. By 1955 the Indian constitution appeared to incorporate some of the most forward-looking laws for women (Gandhi and Shah, p. 18). At the popular level, awareness of the female task-force of the freedom struggle helped bolster the Indian predilection for self-congratulatory exaggeration of actual achievement. Such paradoxes have continued to woo many of those resistant as a rule to change into accepting the belief that there is very little in the Indian woman's position that needs reform.

Moreover, the stridency of many of the Western feminists of the Sixties and Seventies lost them their audience in India. The issues that concerned them were the outcome of an ongoing socio-intellectual debate to which events like the wars had given an added thrust and direction. The West, moreover, had been through innumerable emotional and psychic shifts—mood barometers which reflected the spirit of revolt *against* tradition through manifestations of philosophies like absurdism, existentialism, the modernist *angst*, and so on. Whether these sensibility-shifts were commonly shared or not, they did ultimately consolidate the growing power of another ideology that had been shaping the Western consciousness for some time: individualism.

The importance of individualism in distinguishing between the two world-outlooks, the Western and the Indian, cannot be undermined. In spite of a marginal literary move in the Indian languages towards the Western mood-canon in this respect, both Indian literature and Indian culture have remained largely impervious to its message. Whether this is good or bad, right or wrong, belongs strictly to the realm of normative value-discourse and would ultimately depend on the prevailing ideology (of the individual). At the same time, ideology itself can only be meaningful in relation to a specific context.

The 'spectrum of thinking' or the 'social consciousness' of a given society at a given time is characterized by three connected but distinct segments. These are the segments of intellectual endeavour, common sense and belief, and what may be best described as the collective unconscious.

The connections between the first two of these segments are clear. Today's world of common-sense has been shaped and moulded by the world of intellect of the previous era, and today's intellectual categories will become the cornerstones of tomorrow's commonsensical, widely-accepted social perceptions and understanding. In other words, the accepted norms and boundaries demarcating a people's mind at a given point of time have an evolutionary history. The process begins with the seeds of ideas, largely confined within the intellectual world, which germinate and take root in the popular consciousness over centuries. The third segment, that of the collective unconscious, by and large excludes reason and rationality and primarily consists of faith and deep-rooted emotions.

The difference across cultures, to the extent relevant to the subject-matter of my book, is to be sought in the degree of interconnectedness of these three segments and their power to bring about or resist change. In today's world, the first segment, to a very large extent, shows only minor variations across different cultures, and is overwhelmingly dominated by what could be loosely termed as the Western ideal, i.e. one based on individualism. One of the important characteristics of this mode of thinking is the vision of a technology-driven society where ever-increasing material, and by implication spiritual, freedom for the individual is the cherished goal.

It is important to note that while modern technology is of recent vintage, starting with Hobbes's *Leviathan*, philosophers and social scientists of the Western world with views as diverse as Mill, Weber, Nietzsche, and Marx have grappled with the apparent dichotomy that exists between the individual as an individual and the individual as a social being. The resultant political perceptions, and the definitions of *man*, have differed in the extreme—from that of a solitary individual abstracted from society to one where class identity is the foremost criterion. However, it is individual freedom within the boundaries of necessity that has been a common thread running through all their variant concerns.

This long intellectual pursuit is still alive, and an active area of inquiry. Its net effect has been the integration of individual freedom, fulfilment, and choice as desired goals in the field of commonsensical perception and thinking. The third segment—the collective unconscious—need not necessarily be an integral part of such thinking but it can, in times of strife, stress, and crises, pose a serious challenge.

In India, mainstream Hinduism as well as the other

religious ideologies have worked in tandem to produce a social order wherein individualism has had no role to play. Nirad C. Chaudhari quotes from W.J. Wilkins the extremely astute observation that 'with the Hindu, religion is not a thing for times and seasons only, but professes to regulate his life in all its many relations.' It does this by prescribing ceremonies, observances, and codes of conduct which are binding on him and his family from before his birth to generations after his death. As Wilkins also points out, the Hindu religion covers issues of individual and national concern, and there are virtually no contingencies for which it has not provided laws (Wilkins, *Modern Hinduism* 1887, p. vi. Chaudhuri, p. 10).

It is perhaps because of this that the three segments referred to earlier do not lead to an integrated whole in the Indian context. For instance, the commonsensical thought segment is moulded in equal measure by the wonders of technology and an unfailing faith in the supernatural powers of godmen and rituals. A mere glance at any daily newspaper, English or vernacular, would bear testimony to this. At a recent International Film Festival of avant-garde Western films (Calcutta, January 1994), held in a newly-constructed cinema-hall replete with modern facilities, the Minister of Culture was compared, in the inaugural speech itself, with Hanumān on the quest of the Sanjivanī[14] plant! One may explain this paradox by pointing out that in India, the basic parameters of life—responsibilities, meaning and fulfilment—are not automatically considered as contained in self-actualization, a natural conceptual off-shoot of individualism. Instead, supra-individual categories such as family, caste, and religious and linguistic identities co-exist with the search for individual freedom. More importantly, they often become the dominant aspects in outlining the trajectory of such a search.

Feminism in the West was born of a way of life essentially defined by the philosophy of individualism which, in turn, is linked to the growth of capitalist values. Fox-Genovese sees the political triumph of individualism as having created a hegemony in which individualism is intuitively associated with the defence of individual freedom. This perverts the only freedom historically possible—that which is socially obligated and personally responsible (p. 7). As a result, Western societies have lost the habit of thinking of 'liberties' in the plural, as implying the rights of communities or groups: freedom, fundamentally, has come to mean the freedom of the individual (p. 60).

In an almost similar vein, hooks sees the ethics of Western society, informed by imperialism and capitalism, as teaching its members that the individual good is more important than the collective good, and individual change of greater significance than social change. hooks sees this cultural imperialism reproduced in the feminist tendency to equate individual successes with change even if the masses of women remain unaffected (*Margin* . . ., pp. 28–9). This is not very different from the popular magazine myth-making about successful Indian women referred to earlier.

The fact remains, however, that Western society by and large accepts in theory the principles of rationality and reasoned argument in its modes of operation within the confines of an 'open society' and 'progress'. This does not mean that there are no perversions of these within the system, or that the system does not have its inner contradictions, only that there is a reasonably strong system of checks and balances to absorb the excesses of individual or group behaviour.

Even if one were to grant, for the moment, that Western individualism is desirable, the distant goal towards which all societies should move, the absence of a similar socio-economic foundation would make such individualism impractical in the Indian context. As already argued, one is speaking of a society whose collective unconscious still operates, at a very fundamental level, on the principles of faith and dogma. If the lot of women here has to change, it would have to be done from within such a context. One is not speaking of shifts in paradigms, but of a whole set of different paradigms altogether. The special relationship of the feminist contradictions and dilemmas to the Indian situation would have to define and shape any agenda for reform. Mere aggression and militancy would be disastrous because Indian conditions are unfavourable for the success of *any* revolution that has its roots in individualistic values. For something as fundamentally iconoclastic as a female revolt, they would be fatal.

Even a cursory analysis of a cross-section of the female population in India's most Westernized city, Bombay, would make this clear. From beggar to bai to housewife, the one common denominator linking these women together is their more or less unquestioned acceptance of their role as male/husband/father-defined. They exist in relation to a particular male principle, and it is their mission to cement that principle. Any proposal to redefine this status quo would have to convince with arguments that are understood within this framework of logic.

This may of course suggest that I see no way out of the present morass except through compromise or a buckling under. I can only qualify such an assessment by saying that I see no easy way out of the situation. While I do not advocate a weak-kneed surrender, I do not want to dismiss the force and power of the social consciousness or its hold on virtually all of us. The outcome of the communist experiment in Eastern Europe is a telling example of the vulnerability of a movement or ideology that underestimates the need to relate the base and super-structure of any process of social change: seventy years of communism have clearly not wiped out the deep-rooted irrationalities dictated by issues such as ethnicity or religious identity.

For more or less similar reasons it would, in my view, be self-defeating for women in India to aim for a head-on collision unless they evolve a method of attack which seeks to penetrate the chinks in the anti-feminist armour. At one of the earliest rallies organized by what was then known as the Forum Against Rape, a veteran CPM activist was rightly sceptical about the highly intellectualized flavour of the slogans of protest. According to her these would have no significance for the majority of the marchers, the *zopad-patti* women, who were accustomed to down-to-earth slogans for more basic demands: better wages and the easy availability of affordable food-grain.

Two points emerge from this statement of hers. The first is that no matter how much feminists may bolster their sense of success by pointing to numbers (this rally has been repeatedly cited as an example of female solidarity against sexual exploitation), most Indian women *at all class-levels* are in fact ignorant about the real focus of protest. The second point, and I regard this as crucial, is that this ignorance could falsify the terms of struggle. The need to create fundamental awareness (not mere consciousness-raising but actual *consciousness-erasing*) is therefore a necessary prerequisite to any agitational approach.

If the Indian response to feminism was a combination of scepticism and opposition, it was because the language of Western feminism was alien, its priorities remote to the workings of the Indian mind. Even the demagoguery of revolution has, ultimately, to be tailored to fit the minds of its task-force. This may be seen in the fact that the West has always had its share of sceptics with whom the militants have had to lock horns. Germaine Greer had hoped that her book would be subversive and draw fire from all sections of the community, stating that if it was not ridiculed or reviled, or if opposing groups of women did not find it offensive, it would be innocuous, a failure (*Female Eunuch*, Bantam Books, 1972, pp. 12–13). Greer's statements make it clear that she anticipated shock and outrage from the conservatives of her own sex—'What they can tolerate is intolerable for a woman with any pride' (p. 13).

Admirable fireworks, but an approach which would be self-defeating in the Indian context. That context is one of historical oppression and exploitation of women, shot through with radical protests against a complex series of denominators (gender and caste being two of them). It is one where burqas and bikinis, female pilots and satis strut and fret their hour upon the stage in a seemingly unending procession.

The kind of fundamental awareness I spoke of as a necessary prerequisite to any agitational approach in India cannot be simply defined, because there are several differing levels of such awareness among different groups of women. Broadly speaking, one may sum up the first principles in the manner of Western feminists: the need to be aware that the situation is man-made and therefore not incontrovertible. This is not as easy as it sounds, because to almost all Indian women, conviction of the unchangeability of social, and especially gender-sexual, injustice amounts to a kind of faith. Phrases like purush-jāti[15] and strī-jāti,[16] to name only two, assert the belief in the naturalness of differences—differences that are not so much biological as artificial constructs perpetuated through doctrine and dogma. These are passed on, as a kind of given, from one generation of women to another, mother to daughter, mother-in-law to daughter-in-law.

Several sociological studies of the situation in the Indian subcontinent have commented on the closeness of the female bonding in the more orthodox social structures (see *Separate Worlds: Studies of Purdah in South Asia,* edited by Hanna Papanek and Gail Minault, Chanakya Publications, New Delhi, 1982). This is not only because the joint family still has a very central role to play in our social life, but because the patriarchal structures by and large exclude male participation in the *minutiae triviae* of domestic administration. The somewhat claustrophobic avenues for education prevent girls from obtaining anything but the most pedagogical details of knowledge. Where young, growing girls in the West would have easy (perhaps natural and desirable) access to knowledge of themselves, their bodies, and the outside world including boys/men, girls in India are strait-jacketed into regarding such freedom as wrong and punishable. They have therefore only other women to fall back on.

The concept of female bonding, which Western feminists emphasized, has operated in societies like ours for a very long time, but its special nature is conditioned by the differences between the individualistic vision of the West and our own perception of community-membership as a basic duty. Such membership may mean an intolerable loss of individual freedom in the Western world-view, while the Indian may perceive it as spiritually fulfilling. I do not think it possible to judge either world-view in absolute terms, but I do consider the difference significant enough to claim that there may be fundamental ways of seeing where the twain shall never meet.

My own experience of the Indian situation tells me that, in most instances, this ingrowing dependence of one generation of women upon an earlier one is far from salutary. It has perpetuated forms of oppression by turning them into categories which define what it means to be *caste as a woman*. In using the term *oppression* here, I have in mind the fine distinction which bell hooks has drawn between *being oppressed* (to her this means the absence of choices) and *exploitation* and *discrimination*. According to her, these two terms describe the collective lot of American women more accurately because most of them do have choices, if inadequate ones (*Margin* . . ., p. 5). Most Indian women are taught by other women that they have no choices, that this oppressive condition incorporates both strī-jāti and strī-dharma.[17]

The body has ceased to be an object of celebration among Indian women. It is a liability, something which has to be concealed, not flouted. Bodily emotions, i.e. emotions triggered off by an awareness of bodily stimuli, are equally suspect. Such inhibitions are curiously reinforced by factors such as education and classism—the idea, for instance, that the 'lower' classes are amoral and dissolute, which is not unlike the sexual stereotype of the black woman (hooks, *Ain't* . . ., p. 52), or the British colonial notion of native (Indian) women as wanton and the Eurasian as a shameful example of the corrupting effect of such sexual depravity on the empire-builders (see M.K. Naik, *Mirror on the Wall: Images of India and the Englishman in Anglo-Indian Literature*, Sterling Publishers, New Delhi, 1991, for a documented study of this theme).

If the body is shameful, it still remains the essential starting-point for modes of contact (the absence of contact, rather) with the external world. In other words, there can be no easy, natural, joyful contact with the world as long as the body comes in the way. Sex is an activity that is not supposed to give pleasure, arouse curiosity or the desire for experience, but an act which is taboo until marriage when it is, by some mysterious process, supposed to become a means of expressing love. In fact, it is doubtful whether love enters into the concept at all. Endurance would be a more appropriate term, another brick piled onto the structure of female martyrdom. Sex in marriage is something a good woman is supposed to endure as part of her strī-dharma because it satisfies a hunger and need incomprehensible to her, part of the mysterious area of difference between her kind and the purush-jāti to which her husband belongs. The several surveys in popular magazines of changing sexual mores among the young must be qualified by the observation that such studies are unrepresentative of even the urban youth and signify, at best, a very minute percentage of college-going boys and girls.

If this arouses the ire of Indian male readers, they should look deep within themselves to see whether this is not something they have in fact observed, if not in themselves then in a reasonably large number of men around them, and in their women too. How many men and women would share the 'off-colour' jokes which many men are fond of narrating to their own sex? This is not to suggest that such jokes are a sign of liberation, only that as long as they are considered strictly male property they are most definitely anti-liberation. They imply that smut's comic potential is only perceived by men. By inference, therefore, women don't find sex funny, are unable to appreciate its wild side, cannot participate in a lusty enjoyment of its comic distortions. It is another matter, altogether, that most of these jokes/stories show women in a poor light and are therefore themselves signs of sexual exploitation.

Something of the inhibiting power of the woman-to-woman bonding may also be seen in the kind of sexual ignorance many women grow up in. In the convent-school I attended, sexual knowledge was imparted through whispered, exaggerated explanations to girls who were shocked, at fifteen or sixteen, to learn that babies didn't just 'happen' after marriage. I knew someone who went to the United States after doing her Master's in Bombay. When she arrived there, her periods ceased for several months, as happens to many women during periods of emotional stress and insecurity. Eventually she went to see a physician and told him this. His first question, naturally, was whether she thought she could be pregnant. To which she, in all innocence, actually said, 'I don't know.'

Now what she meant by the words was very different from what the doctor understood her to mean, because this woman was astoundingly ignorant about the biological process by which one could get pregnant. The doctor's subsequent queries about when she thought conception could have taken place made absolutely no sense to her. Eventually the poor man found himself having to explain the facts of life to this twenty-three-year-old Indian woman, and what she heard that day traumatized her for a long, long time. Among other things, she found it difficult to forgive her mother for having kept her so completely in the dark.

This woman may of course have been an extraordinary exception even for my generation, for there were plenty of willing informers even around one's all-girls circuit. But the details could be both garbled and horrifying, especially if one's natural curiosity as a child had been reassuringly satisfied with deceptive answers which left out the biology of sex altogether, and one's growth to adolescence had bodily phenomena covered in a shroud of ugly, shameful secrecy. Though many schools today impart some amount of sex education, the basic attitude of its being not quite respectable has done little to eradicate the furtiveness with which most growing boys and girls regard it.

The secretive manner in which all aspects relating to female sexuality are glossed over in India should make it apparent why some of the obsessions of Western feminists would not apply very readily to our situation. For example, Germaine Greer had listed certain categories in *The Female Eunuch*: Body, Bones, Curves, Wicked Womb, Stereotype, Baby, The Girl, etc. Each of these had posited a step forward in her thesis about the deliberate emasculation of womanhood. As Greer herself had argued, chromosomal difference is meaningless unless it is shown as expressing itself in personality-gender development, and such development cannot take place in a vacuum (p. 5). Greer's purpose was to examine whether the bias about what constitutes femaleness is conditioned and therefore questionable.

Nearly twenty years earlier, Simone de Beauvoir had raised the same issue when she had distinguished between the two terms *female* and *feminine (The Second Sex,* Penguin, 1977, pp. 13–15). As Simone de Beauvoir had emphasized, the distinction was between a biological condition (the female) and a socially imposed concept (the feminine), both of which had somehow become hopelessly entangled so that it was impossible to see the first as separate from the second. As feminists have argued since, the second was often perceived as the primary characteristic of womanhood, the factor which determined social codes of conduct for women.

While these are universal categories, different cultures have evolved their own identifiable priorities as to what being a woman means, though the objective, explicitly or implicitly stated, may have remained the same—the exploitation and oppression of women. In Indian society, the normative thrust has increasingly been towards the concealment of the female body. This may be analysed as a literal and metaphorical extension of purdah: since literal purdah ('curtain') denotes various modes of physical constraints on the public display of the female body, metaphorical purdah marks a shift in emphasis to what is socially considered proper behaviour for a woman. This emphasis has withstood the media revolution, and holds sway over the popular consciousness in spite of the determined if dubious onslaught of the advertising industry.

In the traditional Hindu view, human life has been commonly perceived as falling into four successive stages: Brahmachāryāṣrama,[18] Gṛhasthāṣrama, Vaṇaprasthāṣrama, and Sanyāsāṣrama. Each of these was seen as a quasi-entity with its own norms of behaviour, its set of values and system of ethics. The passage of a woman's life may be seen as similarly slotted into different phases corresponding to defined roles: girl-child, adolescent, wife, daughter-in-law, mother, mother-in-law, sowbhāgyavati,[19] widow.

While some of these categories are implied in the Western world-view (Simone de Beauvoir lists a few), I think it may be safely argued that in the Indian set-up these shifts are sharper, and that a woman's life undergoes far greater culture-dominated changes and adjustments from one phase to another. Moreover, the Western view has been defined in terms of a broadly Judaeo-Christian heritage and other historical developments which have affected and been affected by this heritage, of which the growth of individualism is the most obvious example.

A case begins to emerge, therefore, for a more specific look at Indian texts and the traditions these have created. Through such a study, the specific Indian context would, hopefully, become clearer. This study seems necessary because, even today, tradition has produced innumerable contradictions in our social philosophy and practice. Moreover, for reasons indicated earlier, the nature of Hinduism has restricted the potential for revolt. As Nirad C. Chaudhuri has pointed out, any positive disregard of the Hindu way of life was suppressed mercilessly by the most inhuman kind of social coercion, an Inquisition administered, so to say, by a whole society. While there may have been scope for private scepticism, the scale of such private disbelief was far less than disbelief in Christianity among eighteenth and nineteenth century Europeans (*Hinduism*, p. 121). Any resistance to bondage has not merely been sporadic but, frequently, almost submerged in the currents of conservatism and orthodoxy that condition most Indian minds.

Since the mainstream identity is clearly Hindu, the focus would naturally be on the manner in which this identity has been shaped, and its present characteristics. At the same time, besides the majority Hindu, there are the Muslim, Christian, Parsi, Sikh and other female communities, each equally enfolded in their own cocooning texts.

Yet, as I have maintained earlier, it is possible to speak of a certain common denominator which signifies the Indian woman, especially if one looks at Indian society as a holistic community bound by crisscrossing patterns of behaviour and coexistence. I believe that there is such a thing as *Indianness* even though there may be no easy way of defining its essence in matter-moulded forms of speech. Similarly, it is possible to speak of 'the Indian woman' and to see her in the thick of all her troubling complexities.

In examining what constitutes Indianness, the categories I listed earlier would be of some help. Take the category of the girl-child, for instance. Women activists in different cultures have explored what being a girl-child implies. Simone de Beauvoir maintained that one is not born, but rather becomes a woman (p. 295). Through this statement, de Beauvoir expressed a very fundamental truth about the process of conditioning. However, such a statement *per se* can be of no more than marginal interest in a society where the unborn/newborn girl-child has long been an object of fear, disappointment and revulsion. The ongoing media-battle in India against female foeticide/infanticide is a public pointer to what had hitherto been a private act sanctioned and condoned by the community.

The girl-child in India does not 'become' one. She is one even before she leaves the mother's womb. From birth she is an alien, a fact reinforced in later life by the innumerable tragic instances, some reported, a large number unrecorded, of fathers who have not merely refused to let their daughters return to the parental home, once married, but have even coerced them into going back to their husbands in the face of all kinds of brutality.

These and several related features would make the girl-child a rich and revealing subject of study. In a chapter devoted to this theme, I examine some of the constraints implicit in being born a girl and try, so far as possible, to contextualize them. The girl-child moves on to her next pre-ordained role and becomes a wife. In doing so, she loses her identity and takes on her husband's. This may be globally true to a great extent. Yet, as I try to show in a related chapter, I doubt if Western cultures would come anywhere near Bṛhaspati's definition of the devoted wife, the pativratā: she is someone whose state of mind reflects that of her husband. She shares his distress, his delight, grows sickly and dresses unattractively in his absence, and dies when he does (see P.V. Kane, *History of Dharmaśāstra,* Bhandarkar Oriental Research Institute, Poona, 1941, Vol. II, p. 567).

The total emotive and spiritual immersion in the husband's being, implied in such a statement, may not operate in marriages today. Yet, there is something in it which is very endemic to our world-view of the self-effacing role of the ardhāngini,[20] of the sowbhāgyavati, of a woman among other women in a large family, of a mother, and finally a widow. Each of these is replete with a mixture of contentment and deep unhappiness, feelings that are rarely expressed with total spontaneity, suppressed hopes and dreams, untold tragedies.

Interwoven with all these are the symbols of womanhood: purdah, haveli,[21] chudiyaan, mangal-sūtra, kum-kum, sindoor, or even the colour red[22] itself, and so on. As a translator of Marathi poetry, I have frequently found the associational values of these so bound up in the image that any attempt to convey their sense into English becomes an extremely involved exercise. Often, an intense, pathos-heavy usage translates as trite and sentimental, so remote are the worlds of experience of the two cultures.

At the same time, it should be borne in mind that all these symbols constitute a rigid code of bondage which is solely female-circumscribed. It is a grim pointer to our blinkered perception of culture's stranglehold that we see them, without exception, as heavy with suggestions of romance, lyricism, beauty, enchantment, fulfilment, etc. As long as we ignore their darker implications, they would continue as symbols of forms of oppression for a significant number of Indian women.

As the Nineties inch forward, the global scenario seems to have had very little visible impact on the shaping of the Indian woman. As the enormous success of the televised *Rāmāyaṇa* and *Mahābhārata* indicate, the orthodox view of the Bharatīya nārī, an impossibly ideal, lifeless, colourless, oppressed prototype, is still the popularly accepted one. She is an antidote to the corrupting effect of the so-called 'modern', 'liberated' woman who allegedly models herself on the vile prototype that passes for our popular image of women abroad.

This means that any change is first subjected to a framework of values which seeks to preserve the conservative world-view at all costs. For instance, while divorce is not necessarily a formula for freedom, the fact that a growing number of married women is opting for a breakaway from a sham or unsatisfactory or oppressive marriage is not seen as a positive development, an indication that women may perhaps be protesting radically against an unfair system. Rather the divorced woman, without exception, is viewed as 'Westernized' (i.e. amoral) and unmindful of her duty as a good Indian wife. The persistent resistance in all communities to any moves to replace personal laws by a common civil code has a great deal to do with the fact that personal laws permit the enforcement of primitive, patriarchal values. Such resistance reinforces the paradoxes which manifest themselves repeatedly in the operations of the world outside the home. The embodiments of the 'modern' woman—the working woman, the single/divorced woman, the successful/professional woman—are all up against the most fearsome odds.

The kind of situation one is up against even in an academic set-up may be gauged from the sort of routine experience I made in lecturing to my M.Phil. classes on a theme-course entitled the Emancipated Woman. In exploring the history and literature of the women's movement, I used to run aground amidst the babel of contrary classroom view-points, all in conflict with each other. The male response was simply understood if not as easily accepted. Males with slightly left-of-centre leanings clearly saw me as a wishy-washy liberal. On the other hand their more orthodox, even fundamentalist, companions (the substantial majority, alas!) were firm in their conviction that what is *is* because it should be so. 'That's part of our cultural heritage' was the sort of phrase which occurred with depressing frequency.

One would have expected more revolutionary fervour in the women who were, nearly all of them, working women, and college-lecturers at that. Generally, however, they were apt to view the *status quo* as desirable because traditional, and were given to such immature defences as 'Things are not so bad now—my husband makes the tea first thing in the morning.' The number that viewed Mary Wollstonecraft's categories for women as given and indisputable was also alarmingly large. Such women would agree with Wollstonecraft that being 'more observant daughters, more affectionate sisters, more faithful wives, more reasonable mothers' would indeed make us 'better citizens' ('A Vindication of the Rights of Woman', *Woman as Revolutionary*, edited by Frederick C. Giffon, Mentor, 1973, pp. 56–7). They were apt to come up with statements like this one: 'It's what women were made to be. It is a very normal and sensible classification.'

This is hardly the most enlightened of situations in which to contemplate 'change', itself a relative concept. In the Western context the 'base' of the feminist movement is certainly stronger and capable, therefore, of radical incorporations in the 'superstructure'. In India on the other hand, as already noted, scepticism about feminism has been voiced not merely among the public at large, but by activists involved in, for example, the left movement. Ilina Sen refers to left theorist Vimal Ranadive's dismissal of feminist groups and their insistence on the exploitation of women as having its roots in patriarchy. Ranadive actually accuses women's group activists of wanting to keep women away from the common cause, of not wanting them to be politicized (*A Space Within* . . ., p. 2). Clearly, Ranadive's world-outlook will not allow for the earliest of feminist slogans, viz. that *the personal is political*. It was the recognition of the commonness of personal experience that had led to the politicization of the women's movement abroad.

The argument about priorities can thus originate at this fundamental level of ideological fragmentedness. The danger here is that too rigid a straitjacketing of something so basic as women's issues can ignore Sheila Rowbotham's commonsensical reminder that sex and class are not the same (*Woman's Consciousness* . . ., p. 117).

Sen herself argues for the kind of holistic perspective which I believe is essential if any change is to take place, and questions the narrowness of the left standpoint that women's issues do not matter in the context of the larger struggle against class exploitation. Sen insists that understanding the nature of the variant women's struggles is important in order to get a perspective which will more accurately represent the 'aspirations of the generality of Indian women' than most current feminist theory (p. 4).

Awareness of this priority has made the thrust of much of the recent literature more pointed towards and relevant to Indian issues. Among the more challenging studies, that have emerged as a result of this focus, is *Recasting Women: Essays in Colonial History,* edited by Kumkum Sangari and Sudesh Vaid (Kali for Women, 1991). This collection addresses the need the editors felt 'as academics and activists to understand the historical processes which reconstitute patriarchy in colonial India' (p. 1). They admit the obvious limitations of the project in terms of its focus on the middle class Hindu community in north India, and fear the danger of providing 'hegemonic ideologies . . . converging across region, caste and class' (pp. 3–4). As I see it, however, no one study can address itself to all the complexity of Indian womanhood. This does not diminish the validity of a study that defines its scope, provided it offers a means towards solving a multi-dimensional jigsaw-puzzle.

bell hooks has observed that much feminist theory lacks wholeness because it has emerged from the perspectives of privileged women who live at the centre. Theories that serve to include a vaster variety of experience are complex and slow in developing and, at their 'most visionary', formulated by individuals who have knowledge of both margin and centre. One may use a similar paradigm in a slightly divergent context, such as the Indian one.

There is a sociocultural evolutionary process without which all ideological paradigms can offer little not merely by way of explanation but in more concrete terms. While several studies try to assess this sociocultural process, they have remained far too specialized, failing to address more than an audience interested in the academic issue of women's studies. Hence the growing appraisal of women's issues at the level of disciplined study is rendered counter-productive at the larger level of social apprehension and acceptance. This is because, among other things, the language of discourse has been far too abstruse by common (used in a non-pejorative sense) standards, which in turn has affected its accessibility.

I would want this book to shake its readers, Indian men and women, out of their complacency—to agitate them enough to *reconsider* things they have taken for granted, even if they are some way from being *entirely convinced.* That is why it has seemed necessary to locate my arguments by reference to a tradition which has a direct bearing on our present. That is why, again, I have as far as possible avoided the use of theoretical terms and constructs which would only distance the average reader. The themes I discuss are largely relevant to all Indian women, but for reasons which have nothing to do with my subject, the readership for a book of this kind would be predominantly middle class. It is my hope that it would be of interest to a *wider* representation of that class.

It was apparent in the heyday of Marxism that its converts in India had failed to deliver the goods—in this instance, a model that would answer the needs of our context while retaining the essence of the struggle against the class society. The danger of too rigid an adherence to the cant of ideology rather than to the spirit of its message can result in farcical excess (particularly when such cant becomes a substitute for everyday discourse) as well as in a self-induced deafness on the part of the opposing ideologue. The average readers to whom I may seem in opposition have the conviction of their own ideology and cant. To confront either with an alternative form of cant is an exercise in futility. In any case, the jargon of ideology would only be meaningful to the initiated. It is self-evident that such a category does not exist, except in a marginal sense, in India.

Gandhi and Shah write of the increasing attempts to educate people into an awareness of their responsibility as a community towards women who are victims of domestic harassment because of dowry. There are signs of organized revolt in divergent grass-roots contexts, ranging from the saathins of rural Rajasthan to the women of an urban slum like Dharavi (Bombay), which seem to address issues outside the purview of a purely-middle class existence.

The feudal hierarchies attacked, however, are implicit in Indian society as a whole. In arguing that these must first be eroded within the middle classes, I am not undermining the validity of such movements (or of studies of them) but insisting, rather, that without middle class conviction of their soundness they would remain marginal in their impact.

As of today, rightly or wrongly, it is the middle class in India which controls the weapons of change. It is here that the sensibility-shift must be seen as desirable, and the fallacies of the orthodox view of Indian women understood. The middle class world-view may be interpreted as broadly 'Indian'. It is one which is defined in terms of family and community. Commitment and responsibility to both are an essential part of this view, and both in turn are visualized in the context of tradition. It is a tradition which is broadly negative in its approach to women, but its fundamental priorities differ so widely from the Western approach that they need ultimately to be tackled in context. It is also a tradition whose hold appeared to cut across class-barriers. Strī-jāti, it would appear, had over the centuries acquired a kind of common denominator which retained the margin-centre dialectic within its unity of experience.

Scholars appear to agree on the fact that most

women-related strictures (e.g. the age at which a girl was to be married off, inter-marriages etc.) initially applied to Brahmins alone. The practice was therefore casteist and sexist. However, this would appear to have been diluted over the centuries, so that the caste-factor was replaced in its entirety by the sex to create a new jāti altogether: the female-jāti.

It should be noted that very few other ancient Hindu practices have been allowed to blur caste-differences so wholly, and without arousing any apparent protest. The patriarchal thrust alone would seem to have had universal sanction. For women in India at any rate, gender has become a curious equalizer. The gender-paradox lies in this, that while it is the lowest common denominator at virtually every level in the social structure, the conventional caste-factor has not diminished its hold on social operations. While Marxist ideology would posit that women are twice discriminated against in any class-society, in India the discrimination against them would be by and large three-fold: sex-based (strī-jāti), caste-based (jāti), and class-based. To be *caste as woman* in India is to live out this triple-layered existence.

Chapter 2

Gaurī-Kanyakā-Kumarī

(The Girl-Child)

Discrimination between the sexes in India begins at birth, or even before it. It starts before the child is born, in the mother's womb. None of the conventional blessings showered upon a pregnant woman mentions daughters. It is doubtful whether one would actually exhort a woman to be 'the mother of a hundred sons' in today's India, except in a jocular vein: the emphasis on family planning has made *that* blessing a somewhat dubious one. But exhort her to have at least *one* son, preferably the *first-born*? No well-wisher, it would seem, would admit to wanting anything else.

My own pregnancy was shot through with incidents that pointed to this compulsive obsession with male children. A beggar at a traffic-light began by blessing me with the words '*Daan do, tumhe beta ho jaayega*',[1] but changed her tune to a threatening '*Beti ho jaayegi*'[2] when I failed to meet the expected degree of generosity. The telephone-operator at work burst out with a wholly spontaneous 'How sad!' when I told her I'd had a girl. Several people consolingly said, 'Never mind, better luck next time!' The hospital nurse beamed when my obstetrician said I could start planning another baby if I wanted to. 'Good! she exclaimed. 'Now dream of a boy every night!'

Except the beggar, all these people had heard me say, over and over again, that I wanted a daughter. Yet, all of a sudden, they were starting to eye me pityingly. My protestations were brushed off with a smile that clearly said, 'Sour grapes!' When I seemed in no hurry to have a second child, several people told me I should try, 'at least once' for a son.

A woman in India is made to feel morally obliged to bear a son. Her married life, even today, may be a round of frustrating pregnancies. It was not uncommon about ten years back for people to snigger at families with several daughters: poor things, they'd been trying so hard for a son but all God seemed to have given them was daughters.

While this desire for a male child has been found in virtually all known cultures, it has assumed varying intensity and significance through human history. Its obsessive presence in contemporary India is part-historical and partly sociocultural. It underscores the unchanging priorities of social life and erupts in a cyclical pattern of the most primitive kind. The present-day spate of female infanticide and foeticide are only two of its more extreme forms of current manifestation.

Thus if the brood-of-daughters scenario mentioned earlier is less common today, it has its sinister reasons. There is an ongoing battle between those who argue in favour of the medical need for the continuance of amniocentesis tests and those who point to the evidence that these are used by several urban couples to determine the sex of the unborn child and terminate the pregnancy if it happens to be a girl. Women activists, and those who support the women's cause, have been agitating for a ban on a medical practice that is rapidly degenerating into an eye-wash for female foeticide. A *Times of India* report (2 May 1993) alleges that the increasing abuse of amniocentesis, along with female foeticide and infanticide, and the facility of preselection of sex through spermosorting could mean that in about twenty-five years, the ratio of females to males in Rajasthan could be a mere 1:3. This is only one of the several media warnings that appear to have no effect on the general Indian way of seeing.

In his *History of the Dharmaśāstra*, (Bhandarkar Oriental Research Institute, Poona, 1941, Vol. II, p. 509), noted Sanskritologist P.V. Kane disputes Westermarck's claim that infanticide was prevalent in Vedic times. Kane interprets controversial passages, like *Ṛg Veda* II. 29.1 ('cast off from me sin as a woman who secretly gives birth to a child [casts it off]') as being a reference to the exposure of illegitimate children rather than the murder of a child born in wedlock.

Kane also quotes from the passage which European scholars like Zimmer and Delbrück have used to support their thesis of infanticide: 'They go to the avabhṛtha (the final sacrificial bath); they keep aside the sthālīs (pots) and take up the vessels for vāyu: therefore they (the people) keep aside the girl when she is born and lift up (i.e. greet with pride and joy) the son.' (*Taittirīya Saṁhīta* VI. 5.10.3).[3] According to Kane, this passage means only that the birth of a daughter was not greeted as joyously as that of a son, and cannot be construed as a reference to exposure or infanticide.

It is worth noting however that, by implication, the term *infanticide* is here used to refer exclusively to *female* infanticide—a revealing detail, for it suggests that infanticide need only be construed as gender-based. Similarly, in spite of Kane's vehement rebuttal of its existence, he does not appear to think it necessary to question his own observation, viz. that a son was more desired than a daughter. He actually uses this observation to challenge the existence of a related sexist practice—female infanticide—in ancient Indian society.

The fact remains that gender infanticide was common practice in several cultures. Simone de Beauvoir has pointed out that though orthodox patriarchal regimes give the father absolute control over the lives of his children, social practice usually limits this power in the case of the male child: 'every normal newborn male is allowed to live, whereas the custom of exposing girl infants is widespread' (*Second*, p.114). Maintaining that daughters have been the primary victims of infanticide everywhere, Adrienne Rich refers to Lloyd de Mause who has argued in a documented essay that killing female children was 'routine practice' in medieval Europe and that it was probably responsible for the statistical imbalance of males over females. A husband of the first century BC instructs his wife thus: 'If, as well may happen, you give birth to a child, if it is a boy let it live; if it is a girl, expose it.' (Adrienne Rich, *Of Woman Born: Motherhood as Experience and Institution,* W.W. Norton and Company, New York, 1976, pp. 185–6).

Such infanticide could hardly have been absent in our culture given the other available evidence, then as now, of both the way in which the female sex has been devalued and the preferred status of being the mother of sons rather than of daughters. The matter-of-fact way in which this practice continues in parts of India even today suggests a sustained history rather than a sporadic aberration born of circumstantial need. Except for the occasional outcry in the media, it is shrugged off as not worth bothering about. According to a *Times of India* report dated 23 August 1992, the methods used to murder female infants include feeding them with the milky extract of the erukammpal shrub or with paddy grains in hot milk. A new-born may also have its face covered with a damp towel and then be turned over; drowned in a bucket of water; smothered with pillows; fed pesticide; or overdosed with sleeping pills (Pushpa Iyengar, 'Girls in Salem Are Born to Die').

The same report quotes a female doctor, Dr R.N.V. Manonmani, who runs her own hospital in Rasipuram: 'I support the policy of female infanticide and refuse to admit that it is a sin . . . These mothers have suffered so much that they don't want the pattern repeating in their daughter's lives. They are not committing murder . . . .'

The kind of rationalization implicit in this statement has its roots in a closed-minded conservatism for which our ancient texts have provided enough fodder. It may even be stated in less damning language but its rationale remains dubious. Couched in the guise of empathic understanding, it condones and perpetuates gender-injustice. In support of his interpretation of the passage from *Taittirīya Saṁhitā*, Kane quotes from other sources more or less contemporaneous with it: 'the wife is indeed a friend, the daughter is distress (or humiliation), the son is light in the highest heaven' (*Aitareya Brāhmaṇa*,[4] 33.1); 'the son is one's self, the wife is one's friend, but the daughter is indeed a difficulty' (*The Mahābhārata*, Ādi.[5] 159.11). According to Kane, these sentiments echo those from the passage in *Taittirīya Saṁhitā* referred to earlier—more particularly, they support his interpretation of them as implying that a son's birth received more prominence than a daughter's (p. 510). The highly distressing flavour of these statements, which are unambiguously damning of daughters (and, therefore, of women) merits no comment. He does not appear unduly worried about their implications in the context of gender-discourse, clearly seeing the implicit discrimination as an indisputable given.

Kane even refers to what Bāṇa[6] has king Prabhākaravardhana[7] say about his daughter. Bāṇa's king refers to *this rule of law laid down by someone*, viz. that the daughter one has fondled and cherished becomes another man's (her husband's) one day, and says that it is this knowledge that makes *the good* shed tears when a daughter is born to them (p. 150).

The arbitrariness of the approach is evident from the fact that the *rule of law* owes its existence to no sounder reason than that it was *laid down by someone*. It is fallacious to insist that its operation in varying forms in nearly all known cultures is proof of its incontrovertible logic, for 'the makers and sayers of culture, the namers, have [always] been the sons of the mothers' (Rich, p.xi). What is more disturbing is the fact that, through the ages, there has been a selective nurturing of precisely such pronouncements, which were calculated to preserve a girl/woman's inferior status.

Kane's own response to Bāṇa merely explains the rationale for his stand. According to him, the reason a daughter's birth was not welcome was not because she was not loved but because she was a source of anxiety. Parents dreaded the kind of high moral expectations society placed upon women, and were anxious not to have a daughter because they would need to be perpetually concerned for her reputation and well-being (pp. 510–11).

From here it is only a few steps to the logical justification for female infanticide which even a female doctor in the 1990s can offer. In none of these approaches is there any apparent censure of a society which imposes such unfounded and unjust gender-mores. Instead, there is an unconditional acquiescence in their existence. Moreover, while Bāṇa's king (and by implication, the poet himself) attempts to give us some sort of a reasoned argument as to why a daughter's birth occasions sorrow, it is highly improbable that these thoughts enter into the general atmosphere of gloom surrounding a female birth today.

It is clear that the birth of a daughter is a let-down in some absolute sense. A woman who bears a son, on the other hand, is exalted as someone who has fulfilled her mission as a female. She herself is conditioned into experiencing a sense of achievement at having done so. If the other aspects of bearing a daughter (her presence being temporary and therefore an alleged source of grief) enter the picture at all, they do so at a later stage. Moreover, they are wilfully regarded as an unalterable situation and, in this way, the whole boy-girl child syndrome is perpetuated and rationalized.

Moreover, even if we concede that the girl is an alien in her father's home, it is man-made laws and social strictures that make her so. Right from birth, a girl is made to feel like a bird of passage in her father's home. Even allegedly liberal Indians are prone to harp on facts like dowry, marriage, security, vulnerability etc. as reasons for a parent's greater sense of liability as regards a girl-child. This becomes an explanation of the consequent reluctance to have one at all. Kane had maintained (p. 511) over fifty years ago that a girl's character becomes a source of anxiety, but most teenagers even today would be familiar with the constant parental warning that a girl's reputation is her most precious possession.

This warning is hardly peculiar to the Indian context, but its oppressive overtones are considerably sharper in non-Western cultures including our own. Whatever the rationale offered, there is no gainsaying the fact that the typical Indian girl-child is generally a compulsion rather than a choice. She has to learn quite early on that she is a second-class citizen even in her mother's home. If she has brothers, she has to play second fiddle to them. It is she who is roped in to share the domestic chores, she who plays mother to her younger siblings.

Her breaking-in is all the more rigorous if she happens to belong to an economically deprived class, for even in the best of worlds the girl-child's needs are generally regarded as dispensable. This is a fact which television propaganda in recent years has tried to simplistically rectify, but several feminists have commented on the inadequacy of such messages in a society which equates virtuous women with sacrifice and martyrdom, and in which self-effacement is seen as a primary female attribute. The orthodox requirements for the proper conduct of bhojana decree, among other things, that a person had to leave some part of his food on his plate (curds, honey, ghee, milk and saktu or barley were not to be left), and that these remains were to be given to one's *wife, servant or slave* (Kane, p. 769, italics mine).

The assumption that women should *willingly* submerge

even the desire for food until everyone else in the family has eaten has been developed into an imperative which the Indian woman learns to accept from a very early age. A girl-child's share is therefore less than enough in a family where there isn't 'enough' anyway. Her own mother, having been lulled to sleep each night on the song of deprivation, is conditioned to regard this as a female legacy which it is her duty as a concerned mother to impart to her daughter.

Efforts at the official level to try and correct this inherent defect in vision have resulted in a series of government-sponsored messages on television. In one of these, a pregnant woman is shown dutifully plying her husband with a whole variety of food. 'And what about you?' booms a stentorian voice in the background. In reply, she smilingly holds up two dry rotis—the stereotyped image of the good wife who can subsist on next to nothing as long as her husband is well-fed. 'No!' booms the voice again, 'You have to think of the life in your womb. Your children will be healthy only if you are.' Cut to a shot of the woman chewing vigorously, if unconvincingly, on the good things of life herself. She has the contrived air of someone trying to show you she knows better now.

Even at the most obvious level, one could question this emphasis on the woman as a *mother* rather than as *human being*. In another similar message, a mother pulls her daughter's hair callously when her brother cries, accusing her of having been mean to him. She then calls out to the boy, and fondly heaps his plate with food. The next shot shows the little girl staring sadly at *her* share: two dry rotis, naturally. A voice in the background reproachfully urges the viewers not to treat *their* daughters in this way.

Both these messages are part of the government's attempt to change our social perception of the girl-child and of the Indian woman. It is doubtful whether they have any effect on our fundamental assumption that the female is, at best, the second sex. It is simplistic to expect such superficial moves to mean much in a context where consideration for the woman or the girl-child plays no part in the overall scheme of things. One can safely assume that even among the policy-makers, the general vision of a woman's role remains unchanged. While paying lip-service to a more progressive approach, social practice by and large would create a dichotomy between the message on the television-screen and its relevance to the way individuals conduct their personal lives. Few men/women would admit its applicability to their relationship with/as wives, sisters or mothers. The all-pervasive implications of the message can only be appreciated if it follows on a more basic 'preparedness', a subtle change in consciousness. That change is not yet part of our social reality, whereas the two-dry-rotis syndrome described earlier certainly is.

The rotis are only a tangible symbol of a discrimination that operates in innumerable other ways, as it did with Shanti. She was one of the several girls I used to play with in the little Konkan village my father came from, and where we holidayed every summer. She was fourteen then, and had dropped out of school three or four years earlier. She had a twin-brother who, however, still went to school.

Shanti was ostensibly the family's darling, the only daughter in a family with three sons. She was spoiled and petted by everyone in the family, more fortunate than many of the other girls in the village. Yet, according to her, she had stopped attending school because she didn't need to study or to be able to read. Her brother did: he wanted to pass his 'Matric' and get a job in Bombay. *She* didn't need to get a job—what would people say if she did? They would say her father wasn't able to look after her needs. Her parents would never be able to find a good match for her.

When I once asked Shanti if she didn't want to do something with her life, she got very huffy and asked me what would happen when she got married. 'Who's going to let me do something else then? If I get married at all, that is. If I *do* something, who knows if anyone in my community will marry me? They will all say I am too full of *rubaab*.[8] This way at least I won't enter my husband's home like an uncouth bride who knows nothing and whom everyone can abuse. This is my path. I'm a girl. Girls aren't meant to study. I don't know what you're talking about.'

We battled this theme out every afternoon, sitting on the stone steps in the veranda. What distressed me was not the cheerfulness of her disposition, but her unquestioning acceptance of a collective consciousness and the blind submission to generations of conditioning. I was not much older myself, and often impulsive in my responses, but I did not need a battery of feminist arguments to sense that Shanti typified a situation that those opposed to change could glorify as being a state of contentment and satisfaction. Later, when I graduated with English Honours, a stray passage from Jonathan Swift stuck in my mind: 'the serene, peaceful state of being a fool among knaves'. Shanti was married by then, but I doubt whether she'd have got much joy out of Swift even if she wasn't.

The various conversational mazes down which Shanti and I wandered cannot be easily recaptured and would probably make tedious reading. She was and is even today an example of the way in which conditions are seen as fixed. In her world-view, a girl was unchangeably slotted. She went to school as long as she was able to, more as a diversion than because of any conviction about the need to learn. When it stopped being a diversion, she didn't go any more. The revolutionary possibilities of education didn't enter the picture. She accepted the fact that her brother could control *his* lifestyle, but not she hers. She prepared herself for the ultimate goal—marriage—and groomed herself in a way that would make her transition from daughter to wife as smooth as possible.

Writing of the situation in France in the first half of the twentieth century, Simone de Beauvoir had noted the role of conditioning in the way a girl was seen to develop. Referring to the so-called feminine attributes often observed even in very young girls, she had argued that these were the result of relentless indoctrination from the early years rather than evidence of a mysterious, predetermined push towards 'passivity, coquetry, maternity' (*The Second Sex*, pp. 295–6). The concerns of feminism make it obvious that this indoctrination still operates in almost all cultures. At the same time, the extent to which this is unalterable varies.

Implicit in all Shanti's responses was her conviction that her role as a girl (i.e. a gender-based one) was unconditionally defined whereas her brother's (as boy-man) depended on what he wanted to do. He had the choice, the potential and the power to change. This, in itself was a radical progression from the older world-view which would have seen him as irrevocably doomed to life in a far-from-prosperous village, but its range of vision was clearly restricted to gender-casting from which she, as a woman, was excluded. The power to change, where conceded, is, as with Shanti, commonly perceived as a male prerogative and, in turn, demarcates other social constraints and differences.

Change may be resisted for a variety of reasons. Those who oppose interference in the personal laws of communities generally fear the loss of power which such change can bring about. Resistance to change can also result from a fear of what the brave new world can bring, or the unwillingness to face a hostile group that supports the old world-order. Thus, in the Konkan village referred to, an old woman endured the most excruciating headaches because she feared that wearing glasses would make her seem, of all things, uppity even though several old men in the village who wore them merited no comment. The fact is that no woman of her class in the village had yet worn glasses, either because they hadn't been needed or because they were seen as not necessary for *women* with failing eyesight. If something so non-threatening as *spectacles* could pose such an obstacle in the context of sexual prejudices, the more fundamental moves for change would require a shake-up that seems almost too formidable to contemplate.

Those who resist change may argue that such change could leave its beneficiaries without any moorings and, in fact, prove harmful to them. This theme has been variously handled in Indian literature, but I have chosen here to look at a novel in English—Rama Mehta's *Inside the Haveli* (Arnold Heinemann, 1977). In making this choice I am trying to emphasize that the mere use of a language (English), in which there was by then a tradition of feminist revolt, need not assume a difference in approach.

In this novel, the protagonist Geeta has entered the haveli after marriage, and is initially very much in revolt against its gender-mores. Even in Geeta's so-called rebellious phase, however, her position is never very clearly defined, suggesting as it were a degree of uncertainty on the novelist's own part. When Geeta attempts to send a young servant-girl, Sita, to school with her own daughter, the common haveli response is that she is actually doing the girl a disservice. She is exposing her to a vision of horizons which normally remain inaccessible to the working class, thus running the risk of making her a misfit among her kind.

If this apprehension is understandable at one level, it also underscores the fact that individual gestures remain powerless as long as they are not backed by community support. The personal may be political under certain given conditions but it would need to be politicized in a very fundamental sense before conservative structures are affected in others. This is apparent in Geeta's own feelings of self-doubt and her inability to overcome them, both of which are less easy to accept than the reaction of the other women in the haveli.

Geeta actually seems to echo the sentiments of the servants, and agonizes over the awfulness of her initiative in sending Sita to school. Worse, when Sita is engaged to be married, it is agreed that she would have to stop going to school—a view Geeta acquiesces in just as readily. Eventually therefore, one is left feeling not only that Geeta's move has achieved nothing but that her own stand seems confused and shaky. She surrenders here, as elsewhere in the novel, to the forces of conservatism which confront one everywhere in the Indian situation.

Such conservatism ensures that the girl-child grows up with the conviction that her fate is unquestionably different and less colourful than her brother's. Simone de Beauvoir had observed that till about the age of twelve, young girls were as strong as their brothers, exhibited the same mental skills, and were allowed to compete with them in virtually every field (*Second*, p. 295). While this may be partly true in the Indian context, responsibility is something the girl learns to handle from a very young age, irrespective of whether she is a middle-class child, or the bai's daughter helping her with her various jobs, or even the beggar-girl who invariably begs with a sibling or two in tow while her brother does *his* bit by aping a film-star or singing a film-song a few paces away.

The concept of the young girl as mother, as responsible helpmate and mature caretaker is as much part of our ethos, paradoxically, as the negative stars which supposedly reign at the birth of a girl. The theme of the caring young girl has been handled by several writers. In Rabindranath Tagore's *Postmaster,* the lonely postmaster has only Ratan, a young village-girl, to depend upon in his illness. Though only twelve years old, Ratan, who is an orphan, is described as already being doomed to spinsterhood. She does the housework and does not appear exceptional in any way. Her ordinariness is suggested by the nature of her memories which are focused on the most mundane events. Yet, when the postmaster who is away from his family falls ill and wretchedly longs for his home, it is Ratan who rises to the occasion and becomes the mother and older sister the postmaster remembers with such nostalgia. She fetches the physician, looks after the postmaster, and watches all night by his side. As Tagore comments, 'the little girl no longer remained a little girl.'

The protagonist of Bhalchandra Nemade's Marathi novel *Kosla* (*The Cocoon*) speaks of his sisters as being treated in the 'Hindu fashion'. In other words, they were to be self-effacing in their wants, while the elder sisters did everything from braiding the others' hair to cleaning their arses (*New Writing in India*, ed. Adil Jussawalla, Penguin, 1974, p. 120).

If responsibility comes early, it also squashes much that is instinctual. The girl is repeatedly made aware that her time in her father's home is measured, that there is another home that will one day be hers. In the Indian context, where home, family and community are still so significant in one's relationships with the world, the girl-child exists from the start in a kind of 'isthmus of a middle state'. She is told that she would have to leave for her *real* home one day, but she is also taught to sense that the other place is a hostile one where happiness is chancy, perhaps never to be found.

Paradoxically, once she goes to the other place, her mother's home becomes a symbol for the one place where she can be herself. She acquires a sort of proprietary right to her mother's home, though her welcome there is constrained by the fact of her having another home to which she must unconditionally return. It is to her mother's home that she comes during childbirth and for various important festivals, but her doing so depends upon her 'other' home being agreeable to the idea. Any privileges she enjoys on such occasions are implicitly of a temporary nature. Her allegiance is viewed as being given over to the marital home even if she is an eternal outsider there.

Several literary and popular manifestations of these paradoxes may be found, especially in regional literatures. *Jaa muli jaa, dilya ghari tu sukhi raha* ('go, my daughter, may you be happy in the home you've been given to'), says a popular Marathi song, supposedly sung by the bride's mother on the wedding day, capturing the idea that with marriage a girl is literally 'given away', not merely to her husband but to another household.

A poem by Marathi poet Lakshmibai Tilak[9] describes a maternal aunt's emotions when she goes to fetch her young niece home (i.e. to her mother's house) for one of the most significant among Indian festivals, Diwali. The entire poem is filled with the nuances of Indian girlhood. The young child-bride's life is described as having been shackled by the adults who had married her off. She stands forlorn, a pot of water on her head, listening to a train rattling away in the distance, wondering if anyone from her mother's home will come to take her away for Diwali.

The aunt tries to picture the young girl's thoughts of her mother's home and of the freedom she would enjoy there. Though written in the early part of the twentieth century, the kind of picture the poem evokes remains by and large unchanged. In Marathi, my mother-tongue, the phrase *Jaavayachi baiko* ('the son-in-law's wife') is often used jocularly to refer to the daughter, but it emphasizes the tacit assumption that the daughter is an alien.

Along with this sense of the 'other', one also finds a very clear discrimination between the rights and privileges of a daughter and son. Manu[10] gives daughters only an occasional mention in the rights of inheritance, and in 4.184–85 of the *Manu-Smṛti*[11] it is the wife and son who are seen as part of the householder's body, while the daughter is regarded as 'the supreme object of pity' (*The Laws of Manu,* tr. Wendy Doniger and Brian K. Smith, Penguin, 1992, p. 91. All further references to Manu relate to this edition).

From earliest times, the gender-distinction was operative in several respects. Girls were denied education and knowledge of the scriptures. They were thus kept in purdah long before the practice of physical purdah became a social reality. Secrecy as regards knowledge clearly meant that women had no part in policy-making. Nor were they in a position to question man-made strictures or argue against a position with any strength or conviction. The insistence on a past where women were equal and respected is of little consolation, even if factual evidence concedes it, in the context of our injustice-riddled present.

The intersection of other cultures with the predominant Hindu one did nothing to correct this anti-woman sensibility. Instead, each in turn absorbed and strengthened the areas of commonness in this respect. Neither Islam nor the Judaeo-Christian traditions have distinguished themselves by any manifestation of concern with equal rights and privileges for the two sexes. On the contrary their pronouncements asserted, in various ways, the need for stricter control over their women.

According to Manu, no female—whether girl, young woman or old woman—was to be allowed independence of action. A woman was to be under her father's control in childhood, her husband's once married, and her son's when widowed (5.147–8).

Nothing could be clearer or more damning. From the very beginning, the daughter's role was a non-role in the scheme of things. In the passage just referred to, the term, 'daughter' is not even mentioned. It is hardly surprising, therefore, that both women and men were so fanatically anxious to give birth to a son. Several smṛtis even warn against choosing a brotherless girl for a wife.

There are plenty of allegedly sound reasons given in defence of this strange decree. Referring to these, Kane provides his own rationale, namely, that in ancient times, a man without sons could consider his daughter as one. In such instances, it was generally understood that her son would perform various filial obligations in respect of his maternal grandfather but that his own father would have no such claims on him. Nor would the boy be able to continue descent through his father. Kane suggests that this was one reason why men were reluctant to marry brotherless girls (p. 435).

The rather involved implications in this argument suggest that while a father *could* under certain conditions bestow the status and privileges of a son on a daughter, his doing so marked her out as unsuitable marriage-material. In a society which lays so much store by the *son's* obligations to his parents and his honourable discharge of them, the *daughter* who sought to do so had, first, to have a special right conferred on her and, second, was therefore an undesirable choice in marriage. Further, the very fact that the Śāstras permitted a daughter to assume the role of a son under certain conditions implied that the two were seen as different even in filial rather than biological terms—the difference, in turn, implying unequal status.

The reservation as regards marrying brotherless girls ceased to have much influence over a period of time. Kane wryly remarks that 'in modern times the pendulum has swung the other way, a brotherless girl being a coveted prize if her father be rich' (p. 435)! Not so with the injunction that a woman needed to be under the control of the males in the household, which continued to be adhered to.

Since a woman was declared unfit for independence, the question of her being equipped in the way men were with intellectual training did not arise. Manu has no room for women in the elaborate ceremonies prescribed for the initiation of the chaste Vedic disciple. They are rites meant unambiguously for males alone. More significantly, the marriage-rites for women are equated with the initiation-ritual for men and the role of husband as teacher clearly spelt out: 'serving her husband is (the equivalent of) living with a guru, and household chores are the rites of the fire' (*2.67,* p. 24).

In a hard-hitting poem which comments on this code, Marathi poet Bahiṇābāī (AD 1628–1700) proclaims an ironic resignation to her husband's supremacy over her. She renounces her defiant quest for learning because, at her husband's feet, is all the learning she can get. He is the Vedas, he is knowledge. Serving him is her mission in life, her means to salvation. Each new thought in the poem (from which I quote in a later chapter) is loaded with a double meaning, an irony which has reference to the woman's position within the traditional Hindu framework.

Bahiṇābāī, Janābāī, Mirābāī all have a place within this framework. But, as already argued in Chapter 1, they were exceptional individuals, radical even by present-day standards. The basic message was that a woman's inferior status was decreed. In our own world, this dictates the brother-sister equation within a family. The boy's indiscretions and failings, his whims and tantrums, are viewed more indulgently than his sister's. If the family's resources are limited, the girl's education is the first liability. If both son and daughter wish to opt for a more exclusive or expensive vocational course, the boy gets first preference.

Middle-class girls are educated largely as a concession to a superficial social change. Given the new executive culture, a personable wife has become a necessary appendage. Matrimonial advertisements frequently mention at least a BA degree as one of the necessary assets of a would-be bride. Larger numbers of girl-women are now enrolling for degrees as a result, though many leave halfway if a 'good match' is procured. Those who persevere to the finish usually abandon all intellectual pursuits after marriage and settle down to the far more *serious* business of becoming good wives and mothers.

The preference given to boys over girls in matters such as education is hardly peculiar to India. But the extent of the insistence on such discrimination as being historically and traditionally prescribed and therefore indisputable even in the present day probably is. Such sanction reinforces other prejudices and works towards limiting the freedom of choice girls have in most situations. As already argued, the ignorance women were traditionally kept in has had a stranglehold on their ability to contemplate revolt or change. This had made it virtually impossible to challenge prejudices even if these are rationally unjustifiable.

Among these prejudices are those that are based on the biological difference between *male* and *female*, but which are entirely superfluous to biological fact. The attitude towards menstruation constitutes the most obvious example of the way in which a purely biological difference has been manipulated and imbued with unfounded biases.

The mystery surrounding menstruation has been discussed by Sigmund Freud in *Totem and Taboo* (Pelican, 1938, pp. 45, 49). In *The Female Eunuch*, Germaine Greer remarks that although people's responses to menstruation may seem to be getting more enlightened, our fundamental revulsion towards the process is evident from the secrecy to which we condemn it. She refers to the inhibitions women have as regards sanitary towels and the lengths to which they go to conceal the fact that they are menstruating. Greer also comments on the ambivalence felt by both women and men: while women commonly term menstruation 'the *curse*', men express their disgust through phrases like 'having the rag on' (pp. 44–6).

Strictures about the treatment of menstruation are present in nearly all the major world religions. The *Torah* recommends that a menstruating woman be isolated and regarded as unclean for seven days (*Leviticus 15. 19–24*). Further, if a woman bears a *male* child she shall be unclean seven days and shall remain 'in a state of blood purification for thirty-three days', but if she bears a *female* she shall be unclean for twice that period (i.e. two weeks) and in a state of blood purification for sixty-six days (*Leviticus*, *12.2–5*).

In India, the various religious cultures are curiously agreed in their reservations about a simple physical process like menstruation. It is, admittedly, a messy, inconveniencing process which women would gladly forgo if they had the choice, but there seems no justification for the sustained onslaught launched by our law-makers on it. Manu warns a man not to lie in the same bed as a menstruating woman (4.40, p. 78), or even converse with her (4.57, p. 79). Having sex with a menstruating woman makes a man lose his wisdom, strength, sight, energy and longevity (4.41, p. 78). By refraining from such intercourse, he supposedly enhances these qualities in himself (*4.42*, p. 78)! A man who has 'shed his semen' in a menstruating woman is asked to atone for this evil act by carrying out the 'Painful Heating' vow (*11.174*, pp.267–8).

Parsi scriptures also insisted on strict separation of a menstruating woman. The fifteenth section or fargard of the *Vandidad* enumerates certain crimes incapable of being pardoned. These include having sex with a menstruating woman, which is even deemed a capital crime. In the sixteenth fargard, which is concerned with how a menstruating woman should conduct herself, her condition ('illness') is 'directly declared to be the work of the devils'. She has to purify herself (after rigorous separation) by performing the Izashne and Niaish. This involves the placing of three stones, on two of which she must wash herself with cow's urine. The third is where she performs her ablutions with water. After this, she is required to destroy two hundred vermin (John Wilson, *The Parsi Religion,* Vintage Books, 1989, p. 331 [first published in 1843]). Strictures about a menstruating woman are also found in the Koran (*Sura 2.222*).

The West may by and large be assumed to have moved away from the orthodox revulsion regarding the menstrual process, but the historical tradition of suspicion surrounding it is well-documented. Simone de Beauvoir refers to Pliny's view that a menstruating woman ruins crops, destroys gardens, kills bees and turns wine to vinegar. She points out that as recently as 1878, the *British Medical Journal*, no less, reported that 'it is an undoubted fact that meat spoils when touched by menstruating women'. A woman having *the curse* was forbidden entry into refineries in northern France in the early twentieth century on the grounds that she could cause the sugar to blacken (*Second*, pp. 180–1).

The Western context today may however be regarded as several paces ahead of one where a menstruating woman is still forbidden entry into the kitchen and cannot openly and frankly participate in a religious ritual. As a growing girl, I remember being puzzled by a mysterious occurrence which rendered the mothers of several of my friends 'out-of-doors' (a common euphemism to denote a menstruating woman) on certain days every month. Equally mystifying was their state of total segregation at this time, and the fact that they were not allowed to touch anything. Later, when I was initiated into the thing itself, my grandmother, though an exceptional woman in many ways, warned me to make sure my 'condition' never showed. It was nothing to be ashamed of, I was told, but it could make people talk. A fact I discovered for myself soon enough.

It may be argued that these strictures are today honoured more in the breach than in the observance, even in India. This claim would however hold in urban India if at all. Even if the rigours are dispensed with, the general feeling that menstrual blood is somehow polluting and unclean persists. In rural India, where orthodoxy still prevails, the misapprehensions about menstruation would be funny if they weren't also frightening. I remember an old aunt attributing even the appearance of a cobra in the yard to the possible failure of certain menstruating female relatives to observe the rites of segregation and stay away from the kitchen (a charge levelled at my sister and me).

Ours is a context where absurd practices can be held aloft self-righteously as an example of how 'advanced' we were in the history of human thought. A dubious reference to the strictures of Pliny (mentioned earlier) and to Professor B. Schick's discovery in 1920 that menstruating women secreted a toxin (*Menotoxin*) which allegedly made plants wither, can lead to the following self-congratulatory statement: 'It is indeed remarkable how thousands of years ago we recognized the influence of the menstruating women and [*sic*!] environment' ('Menstrual Customs Among the Zoroastrians', in *Jame-e-Jamshed Weekly,* 11 April 1993).

The inescapable fact perhaps is that menstruation, like child-bearing, has been a handy tool for all male supremacist cultures to fashion their prejudices with. Gloria Steinem's tongue-in-cheek review of what would happen 'If Men Could Menstruate' exposes the sexism implicit in the prevalent male-dominated approach to various biological processes (written in 1978; included in *Outrageous Acts and Everyday Rebellions*, Holt, Rinehart and Winston, New York, 1983, pp. 338–40).

Steinem lists several hypothetical corollaries to her theorem: menstruation would become an enviable, boast-worthy, masculine event; men would brag about how long and how much; young boys would talk about it as the envied beginning of manhood, with gifts, religious ceremonies and stag parties marking the day; doctors would research little about heart attacks, from which men were hormonally protected, but everything about cramps; sanitary supplies would be federally funded and free; statistical surveys would show that men did better in sports and won more Olympic medals during their periods; and so on, *ad nauseum*. Steinem wryly remarks that certain things would remain the same: medical schools would use this to reinforce an existing prejudice about admitting women ('they might faint at the sight of blood'). She concludes that even if men could menstruate, the power justifications would still go on and on. In India, however, we are still a long way off even from being able to accept such flippancy about menstruation.

A middle-class girl who manages to transcend various social gender-limitations, does well in school and university, and eventually gets a job, learns all too early that her job is something tolerated for the most part. It is seen as an economic boost in some cases, a matter of pride in some others (particularly if the job is a prestigious one), but very rarely as a serious viable alternative to her *real* vocation in life, viz. marriage. This is why a daughter with a job is never let off her share of domestic responsibility. A son is never expected to help in the routine of domestic chores. Once he begins to earn, he is handled with kid gloves and treated as a creature with special needs and cares. The Western pattern wherein both daughters and sons tend to leave home once they reach a certain age is comparatively rare in India. The girl has to fit in her job outside the house with her jobs inside it—a sort of preamble to the way her life will have to reshape itself always. Her working outside the house is tacitly assumed to be superfluous and dispensable, even if she is professionally successful. It is hardly ever viewed as a possible means to self-fulfilment.

Tagore's poem 'Didi', was a realistic if moving depiction of a little girl from the working class. She is shown running up and down the river-bank, attending to the needs of the labourers digging there. Her feet are weighted down with brass anklets which clank as she moves. Substitute mother, she has a little brother, naked and grubby, who sits on the embankment watching her work. The awesome burden on this child-woman is captured in a passage which describes her, pot of water on her head, food-vessel in one hand and her little brother's hand in the other. Though written about a hundred years ago, Tagore's poem can hardly be called dated. It is a startling statement of a very contemporary scenario.

In 'Five Tongues of Fire', a poem written in Marathi nearly eighty years after this Tagore poem, Indira Sant[12] describes how a daughter's job changes very little in her world. She still remains the older sister of the more conventional world-order described in Nemade's novel which I mentioned earlier in this chapter. Her job is wryly summed up as having to silently accomplish as much as possible before leaving the house. She pays the younger brother's fees, buys a ribbon for her sister, and new glasses for the father. She takes the family to the cinema on holidays, and hands over the bulk of the money earned on pay-day. The boy's job is in obvious contrast. It is fuss and tantrums, his clothes freshly laundered, his tiffin filled with good food. He is allowed to come and go as he pleases. Unlike his sister, he is reluctant to part with money even when he is asked for it.

Most families still feel a sense of irrational horror at the thought of a daughter remaining unmarried even if she is economically independent and seems reasonably self-contained. This phobia is present even in the Śāstrās and may perhaps be traced to the insidious influence they exercise on the contemporary mainstream consciousness in India. Significantly, the Śāstras have no specific mention of the desired or desirable age at which a *man* should marry. Within their framework it is not even imperative that he does so at all: in spite of the gṛhasthāṣrama being an important second phase in a man's life, celibacy was permitted if a man desired it. 'A man could remain celibate all his life, while at least in medieval and modern times marriage has been absolutely necessary for every girl' (Kane, p. 438).

To this necessity was added the need to get her married off at an increasingly early age. That this was a later development may be seen from the fact that the *Ṛgveda* has no definitive statements about the age at which a girl was to be married off, and even seems to indicate that accomplished girls were allowed to choose their own mates. Gradually, however, the emphasis on marrying a girl off before she grew too old became pronounced. Moreover, the definition of what was the 'right' age for this is also, from a contemporary point of view, highly sexist and variable.

A man could marry only after he had finished his period of study, which in turn was variable. Manu exhorts a thirty-year-old man to marry a twelve-year-old girl who charms his heart, and a man of twenty-four an eight-year-old girl

(*9.94*, p. 208)! Kane refers to the *Viṣṇupurāṇa*[13] (III.10.16) which says that the bride's age should be one-third that of her husband, and to the *Mahābhārata* (*Anuśāsana* 44.14),[14] where the same ratio is advocated: a thirty-year-old man is exhorted to wed a ten-year-old bride, and a twenty-one-year-old man a seven-year-old one (pp. 438–9)!

Generally speaking, it was advocated that girls should be married just before puberty or immediately on reaching it. In addition, considerable emphasis is laid on her being a nagnikā. There is no one opinion on what the term means, but the varying interpretations add up to a girl who is about to enter puberty, and who is therefore fit for intercourse. There are even references to the nagnikā as 'one who looks pretty even without clothes' (Aṣṭāvakra, the commentator of the *Mānava gr.*),[15] which would suggest a girl who had not yet physically matured. Elsewhere, as in Gautama (*18.20–23*),[16] it is stated that 'a girl should be given in marriage before she attains the age of puberty. He who neglects it commits a sin' (Kane, pp.440–2).

Paradoxically, in spite of the evidence that marriage at a young age was seen as essential for a girl, some of the statements found in the Śāstras would appear to qualify such a stand. Manu says that while a man ought to give his daughter to a suitable man even if she is too young for marriage, she would be better off unmarried rather than married to an unworthy man. Three years after a girl has reached puberty, she has the freedom to find her own husband if one has not been found for her: in this, neither she nor the man she approaches are to blame (Manu, *9.88–91*, p. 208). Other Śāstras more or less echo these sentiments, but some of them actually maintain that 'the father or guardian incurs the sin of destroying an embryo at each appearance of menses as long as the girl is unmarried' (Kane, pp. 442–3)!

The *History of Dharmaśāstra* has a comprehensive survey of the various pronouncements about the desired age at which girls should marry. The details, which often overlap and even contradict one another, suggest that there was no absolute consensus but that from about AD 200 onwards popular sentiment was in favour of pre-puberty marriages. Kane even attributes this to the presence of Buddhist nuns and an alleged laxity of morals among them! He further maintains that by this time girls were not educated and society did not like them to remain idle.

None of these arguments appear sound enough from even a contemporaneous point of view. It would surely have been more commendable to study *why* the education of girls had been stopped and to try and restore their access to it. Perhaps the more irrational beliefs would provide an answer which if not acceptable would at least be a more convincing explanation. Kane himself refers to the *Ṛgveda* (x.85.40–1) wherein it is maintained that Soma,[17] Gandharva[18] and Agni[19] were a girl's divine guardians. Soma was reputed to enjoy a girl first, Gandharva staked his claim when her breasts developed, and Agni was aroused when she menstruated! The girl was therefore to be married before she developed any distinct signs of femininity (p. 443).

It was even held that the parents and eldest brother of a rajasvalā go to hell if she is unmarried by the time she reaches that stage in her life. Parāśara (VII. 6–9) is quoted by Kane as defining a girl of eight as a gaurī, one of nine as a rohiṇī, one who is ten as a kanyā, and one who is more than this age as a rajasvalā. This suggests that the stage referred to is that of the onset of menstruation. 'If a person does not give away a maiden when she has reached her 12th year, his pitṛs[20] have to drink every month her menstrual discharge', warns Parāśara.[21] Kane maintains that there is nothing absurd in these strictures which were found, in varying forms, in the West as well (pp. 444–6).

This is hardly the best of defences. Moreover, the concern here is not with how globally widespread this practice allegedly was in the past, but with the manner in which practices not merely condoned but advocated as desirable by the ancient Śāstras still continue to mould present-day modes of thinking in India. Kane's argument that such strictures applied only to the daughters of Brahmins and that lesser-born Hindus were exempt from the need to marry young, casteist as the norm is, seems further invalidated in a context where the marriage of the girl-child is a perpetual phobia which has very little to do with her caste.

Child-marriages are still rampant in rural India in spite of punitive laws forbidding them. 'No Minor Offence' by Sakina Yusuf Khan (*Times of India, Sunday Review,* 9 May 1993) alleges that at least 500 child marriages took place in Jaipur district itself on Akha Teej day that year, while in other parts of the state, the number reached a few thousand. All these marriages were in violation of the Child Marriage Restraint Act. Akha Teej is Rajasthan's child marriage festival. Apparently, the low number of such marriages this year was because the authorities were expected to carry out surprise checks. Undaunted, the perpetrators of this practice plan to hoodwink the government by holding the ceremony on another auspicious day!

Those who support this practice have a variety of reasons for doing so, primarily economic ones. Their retrograde views may possibly be the outcome of a closed world syndrome which one almost despairs of hoping to penetrate or change when even middle-class parents are prepared to go to any lengths to get their daughters married off and to ensure that they stay that way. A colleague generally known for his radical bent of mind (he liked to describe himself as a Marxist) was rumoured to have paid his daughter's prospective in-laws a substantial dowry in cash and kind. While this shocked some of us, what was more distressing was the attitude of another colleague reputed to champion the struggle for female emancipation in a minority community, who defended this action on the grounds that there may have been compelling reasons for it which we were unaware of.

The point here is whether a daughter's marriage is so compelling and binding on a man that he is prepared to compromise his own intellectual and moral principles to effect it. The daughter, by all accounts, was educated and had a job. The man himself had had the opportunity to think afresh, with access to some of the most radical modes of ideology and thought. If such a marriage could not produce a sense of misgiving in an allegedly liberal individual, it at least explains why the more extreme cases occur. Here was a man who had the intellectual armoury to challenge the complusion to marry off his daughter at all costs, and who obviously failed to resist the pressure. The sense of paranoia experienced by a more visibly conditioned individual may then be partially glimpsed.

The fanatical need to get a daughter married off today, as well as the conviction that an unmarried girl who is not in the first flush of youth is somehow tainted may be traced without difficulty to the shackling if not wholly conscious hold of the Śāstras and their dubious focus on the female sex. The same sources undoubtedly also have a great deal to do with the conviction that a woman is unworthy of an independent life. Manu rails against the alleged untrustworthiness of women and the need to keep them well-tethered.

It was fairly common for girls from poor families to be married off to elderly widowers. Premchand's[22] Hindi novel *Nirmala* describes the ordeals of its heroine, a young girl who is abandoned by the man she is betrothed to when the death of her father changes her economic situation. She is unable to find another man willing to marry her and suffers the humiliation of being married off to a much older man, a widower with three sons. The novel brings out all the injustice inherent in Nirmala's existence with Premchand's characteristic, unsparing sharpness.

The Marathi play *Sharada* written by Govind Ballal Deval also describes the unhappiness of a young girl when she learns that she is to be married off to a man who is several years her senior in age. Tagore's poem 'Nishkriti' ('Escape') is an ironic commentary on the double standards even fathers have towards their daughters. The father in the poem marries his daughter off to a high-caste Brahmin who is much older than she is even though her mother is against the wedding. When the young girl returns home, widowed, soon after the wedding, the father is outraged when the mother begins talking about her remarrying. All through this long poem, the father is revealed as one who is immersed in what he believes are the tenets of dharma. The word is used to defend and rationalize every retrograde act or opinion. However, when the mother dies unexpectedly, the father thinks nothing of marrying again. This is also in keeping with his dharma as a householder, he tells his daughters. He returns from this second marriage to find that his daughter has run away with her next-door lover, the man she and her mother had always wanted as her husband. In spite of this somewhat revolutionary ending, the entire poem is a hard-hitting critique of the unfair norms constraining the lives of women.

Widowers with grown-up children commonly marry young virgins in rural India even today, without ostensibly arousing either the indignation or protest of the community. On the other hand, widow remarriage is hardly ever heard of, and it is almost inconceivable that it could take place without provoking strong reactions or, at the very least, malicious gossip. The subject of widows in Indian society is another one which highlights continued sexual discrimination of the most abhorrent kind, and is taken up for detailed study and analysis later on.

The age of the bride—and bridegroom—is only one among several other factors which reassert gender-discrimination. The mass of details which specify the suitability of a bride far outweighs those set down for a suitable bridegroom. Kane lists most of the primary sources in the Śāstras which outline the qualities one ought to look for in choosing a bride/bridegroom (pp. 429–35). I give some of these below.

The bridegroom was required to be 'a man endowed with intelligence' (*Āśv. gr.I.5.2*).[23] He had to be of 'good family, a good character, auspicious characteristics, learning and good health' (*Āp. gr.3.20*).[24] These qualities are repeated variously in other texts. Certain kind of bridegrooms are also seen as undesirable. Kātyāyana[25] lists them as 'the lunatic, one guilty of grave sins, leprous, impotent, one of the same gotra,[26] one bereft of eyesight or hearing, an epileptic.' These qualities were also used to disqualify brides (p. 429). However, commentators and law-makers were far more pernickety in detailing the assets of a desirable bride. Besides the common categories, which also applied to the bridegroom, there are elaborate catalogues of physical specifications which do not seem to have held good for men. The *Śat. Br. (I.2.5.16)*[27] maintains that in order to be attractive a female should have broad hips and a slender waist. According to Manu, girls with red hair, physical deformities, either too much or no body hair, a sallow complexion and a sickly physique were to be avoided. He advocates marriage with a woman who is well-formed, has a pleasant name, the gait of a goose or an elephant, fine teeth and hair, and a delicate physique (Manu, *3.8, 10,* p. 44). The *Viṣṇu-purāṇa* (III.10.18–22) adds that a girl should not have a hairy chin or upper lip. Her voice should be musical (not hoarse or like a crow's). She should not have hairy legs or ankles, and should be the right height (i.e. neither too tall nor too short). She is even forbidden dimples when she laughs!

Strictures about softness, daintiness, or excessive hairiness are universal and continue to dominate the social consciousness in several cultures globally. In the West, a 'moustache' was regarded as one of the give-away signs that a woman was a witch. Women themselves have been reduced to a pathetic paranoia about bodily hair and will go to absurd and painful lengths to obliterate every trace of hair, even pubic hair, from their bodies. I remember reading an agonized letter in a women's magazine when I was in college, from a girl who was about to be married and who was worried about the growth of dark hair around her aureoles. The columnist actually advised her to use tweezers to remove it.

There are undoubtedly innumerable macho men who would prefer their women depilated and hairless. At the same time it must be pointed out that the phobia about body hair begins in virtually every girl soon after she reaches adolescence. Greer has observed how hairiness has been associated in the popular imagination with bestiality. Men have cultivated it the way they did competitive and aggressive instincts, while women suppressed it as they did all aspects of their vigour and libido. The fact is that smelly, hairy armpits are as revolting in a man as in a woman. The mean, as Greer puts it, is 'the body cared for and kept reasonably clean, the body desirable, whether it be male or female' (*The Female Eunuch*, p. 31).

The 'psychological sell' which promotes this fastidiousness about female beauty (Greer, p. 81) is reinforced by modern advertising with its emphasis on the potential of female *glamour*. Sleek cars, beautiful houses, seashore resorts, after-shave lotions, all these have long-limbed, smooth-torsoed, sun-bronzed goddesses tagged on as if in natural corollary to the acquisition of these assets. By stripping themselves of natural characteristics to, paradoxically, *accentuate* sexual attractiveness, women are in fact perpetuating the myth of their desirability as being separate from their biology. This is as absurd as the macho image of male desirability. In India, the rite of vadhu-pariksha[28] would take these norms seriously enough for them to become a major source of worry for a would-be bride.

The ancient Indian Śāstras listed other factors besides the physical attributes referred to earlier. Manu (3.9, p. 44) even enlists the sorts of names that make a girl unsuitable as a prospective bride. The *Kāmasūtra* (III.1.13[29]) says that a man should not choose for a bride a girl whose name ends in the *r* or *l* sound. Occasionally, intelligence is mentioned. *Mānava gr.* (I.7.6–7) adds the quality of vidyā (learning) after beauty and before prajñā (intelligence).

Other strictures involved the passing of certain tests such as the selection of lumps of earth. The constitution of the lump a girl selected was supposed to signify her suitability or otherwise. The number of sources which enumerate this practice (Kane, pp. 434–5) suggest that such yardsticks were taken with some degree of seriousness.

The Śāstras are also more or less agreed on the fact that while a Brahmin male could, in certain circumstances, marry a bride belonging to a lower caste, a similar concession could not be made for a Brahmin girl. It becomes apparent therefore that privileges of gender were present even within the privileged caste. The fact that a Brahmin female's union with a non-Brahmin was not accepted as legal is an indication of a way of life born of feudal patriarchy. In varying forms this code may be found in different cultures. Its widespread prevalence shows that notions of the supremacy of the male partner in any male-female relationship are universal and deeply embedded in the human consciousness. In Samuel Richardson's eighteenth century English novel *Pamela,* Pamela's would-be-seducer-now-turned-saviour-husband has very definite views on why *he,* a squire, could marry a servant-girl like Pamela while the idea of his sister's ever being allowed to marry a footman was preposterous. According to him, the husband elevates a wife to his level if better born than her, but drags her down if less fortunate than her in birth! It was therefore important that no woman should marry beneath her!

An inter-caste marriage between a Brahmin male and a non-Brahmin female was not prohibited earlier, though the Śāstras were rather conservative in matters regarding the rights and inheritance-claims of a low-born wife. However, there was general consensus as regards the undesirability of a *woman* of a higher varṇa marrying a *man* of a lower varṇa.

The two kinds of union are even described in two distinct, highly suggestive physical terms. The union of a male of a higher varṇa with a woman of a lower varṇa was described as anuloma, the literal meaning of which is 'with the hair', i.e. in the natural order. The union of a female of a higher varṇa with a male of a lower varṇa was, however, termed pratiloma, literally meaning 'against the growth of the hair', i.e. against the natural or proper order (Kane, p. 52).

It could of course be argued that the Śāstras should be viewed with reference to the time at which they were written. The point is that they seem prescriptive, even in their own time, of a world-order which arbitrarily assumes that women needed certain separate codes. A similar assumption is to be found in certain other practices and attitudes towards women which are frequently explained/defended in the context of the protection of women. The rationale behind terms such as protection/chivalry/shelter with respect to constraints imposed on women is easily if glibly historicized by reference to history and observed patterns of male behaviour. On the other hand, it was hardly ever conceded that the different social purdahs behind which women were confined only served to make them helpless, impotent, and unable to cope with the larger social realities. Along this complex route they were placed in a position of weakness wherein it was natural to see them as needing protection.

What is indisputable is the fact that codes ostensibly developed for the protection of women became, somewhere along the line, instruments with which to exploit and oppress them. Every existing faith that I can think of displays an explicit ambivalence towards women. They were (and are) universally seen as the cause of sin, corruption, destruction and evil. Theological and other canonical texts balance this view of woman with the image of her as weak and helpless. These mould the consciousness of a people until they are as natural to their way of life as breathing. A man-made system is thus instinctually apprehended as the final truth and, in the process, many parallel statements of apparently equal significance are conveniently ignored.

For instance, while the Śāstras spoke of the need to marry a girl off, and to marry her off young, parents were also warned against giving their daughters to bridegrooms with certain defects. Manu even maintained that *no* marriage was preferable to an *undesirable* one. However, while these warnings appear to have been diluted over a period of time, the obsessive need to get a daughter married off has not lessened.

A girl who is getting on in age is often married off to *anyone* who will have her for a price even if the man is blatantly unsuitable. I have known of several such marriages, which usually end disastrously. A female relative of mine was comparatively fortunate, for she was only abandoned by her illiterate husband—though not before she had been accused of being 'ill-starred' and therefore blamed for her aged father-in-law's death as well as her sister-in-law's fractured femur. Other women have had to endure brutal ill-treatment, promiscuity, and daily humiliation by the husband's family, while considering themselves fortunate in having been able to find a husband at all. It would be worth examining the Śāstras to find the authority, if any, which condones such behaviour. One need hardly point out that the absence of such authority has not acted as a deterrent.

The 'protection' syndrome becomes sinister when it sees this as an end-in-itself, because the motives are then questionable and the means adopted to enforce such protection could be insensitive, rigid and often cruel. In *The First Sex* (Penguin, 1978) Elizabeth Gould Davis describes how the idealized code of chivalry had produced such horrendous practices as the medieval chastity-belt.

Medieval women were usually locked into corsets made of silver or iron which had a metal bar curving between the legs. This bar had a very small opening which was enforced with rows of sharp teeth. Only the woman's husband had access to the key. This meant that when he was away fighting wars, as often happened in those times, the woman had to endure indescribable agony. Even basic human functions like relieving or cleaning herself became impossible. Apparently there were many women who killed themselves by jumping off the castle battlements as a way out of this torture (p. 166).

For those who imagine that this barbaric aberration died out with the middle ages and that it was peculiar to 'foreign' cultures, the following account about forms of female bondage in rural Rajasthan ought to come as an eye-opener. The concerted effort of the saathins in this region have exposed at least *some* of the feudal atrocities women are still made to endure.

Among these is the case of Kamli, who was married to a man called Balram, who was twenty years older than her. Balram's jealousy of his young wife made him encase her pelvic region in an iron underwear made by the village blacksmith. This underwear had a waistband with a lock. Balram opened this whenever Kamli needed to relieve herself, and even went with her to the fields on these occasions, but kept her imprisoned in this manner the rest of the time. It was Kamli's brother who discovered how she was being tortured and approached the saathins for assistance. The saathins managed to free Kamli, but she had to be hospitalized for the treatment of the damage done to her pelvic region ('The Second Sex Awakens' by Harinder Baweja, *India Today*, 31 October 1992).

The practice of female circumcision in sections of Indian society and in several Muslim cultures throughout the world is cruelly discriminatory both in the motives behind the act and in the community's attitude towards it. As various activists have pointed out, the term 'female circumcision' is itself deceptive for the process it describes is enormously different from male circumcision. Sue Armstrong points out that the female operation generally means that healthy and very sensitive organs are removed. She refers to the demand made by delegates to a conference in Addis Ababa, viz. that the practice be more appropriately termed 'female genital mutilation' (FGM), which is what it actually amounts to ('Female Circumcision: Fighting a Cruel Tradition' by Sue Armstrong, *New Scientist,* 2 February 1991, p. 42).

A male child's circumcision is supposed to serve the purpose of enhancing sexual gratification, whereas in the girl its purpose is to obliterate all sexual and erotic enjoyment. In *Women and Neuroses*, Nawal al-Saadawi, an Egyptian doctor who was herself circumscribed at six, comments bitterly on the 'irony' implicit in the fact that 'society looks at the woman as a tool of love and deprives her of the one organ which will make her good at it' (quoted by Naila Minai, *Women in Islam*: *Tradition and Transition in the Middle East,* Seaview Books, 1981, p. 99).

The aim of clitoridectomy, ostensibly, is to safeguard the girl/woman's honour, and its distastefully sexist implications are enhanced by the manner in which the boy's circumcision is an occasion for celebration while the girl's is furtive, shrouded in secrecy and shame and illegally performed for the most part. Some of the horrendous methods used to render a girl 'safe' from promiscuity have been highlighted by the media and by feminists.

Gould Davis quotes a passage from Sir Richard Burton's *Love, War, and Fancy; Notes to the Arabian Nights* (London, Kimber, 1954, p. 107) wherein Burton describes some of these. According to Burton, Arab girls who reached puberty had their clitoris and labia majora pared down to the bone with a sharp razor. The two parts were then sewn up with a pack needle and sheepskin thread, a metal tube being inserted to help the passage of urine. The bridegroom allegedly trained himself for a month by means of a strengthening diet to try and penetrate her naturally. Failing this, he supposedly used his fingers or, if necessary, even a knife (*The First Sex*, pp. 156–7).

Nawaal al-Saadawi describes the traumatizing effect of clitoridectomy on herself. Many articulate Indian women belonging to the community abhor the practice but subject their daughters to it all the same, since resisting the community code would endanger their marriage prospects. 'For the girl, *khatna* (circumcision) is not an entrance into the community, nor a positive sign of adulthood; rather, it is a disciplinary action, perceived as necessitated by her maturing. Something to be done, but not to be celebrated' ('Behind the Veil, the Mutilation' by Sandhya Srinivasan, *The Independent,* Vantage, 14 April 1991).

Significantly, according to Naila Minai, the Koran makes no mention of the practice. Minai maintains that the Prophet disapproved of it since it renders a woman frigid for life, but was unable to put an end to it, which may account for the story which claims that he stopped a matron one day from performing the operation on a little girl with the words: 'Reduce but don't destroy.' This has, however, according to Minai, been conveniently interpreted by some Muslims as 'an order to perform the Sunna circumcision on little girls' (pp. 97–98). Sue Armstrong points out that the operation is being performed at an even younger age than was the custom.

The innumerable emphases on a woman's honour as well as the methods and strictures laid down to preserve it mean that as a girl grows up, the burden of shame that accompanies femaleness makes it difficult for her to regard her body as something to be proud of. Ironically, for a culture that lays so much stress on such details of female adornment as jewellery of varying degrees of ornateness, we have a traditional horror against the concept of the body as worthy of admiration. In spite of the unabashed nudity of our ancient sculpture, and paradoxically, in spite of the cholis which form part of conventional present-day attire and are seen by many foreigners as delightfully provocative, the push remains towards concealment rather than display. The extent to which this is so may vary from region to region, and according to religion in some instances, but it is by and large prevalent throughout India.

A basic corollary of this code of concealment is that even today forms of dress could be associated with moral values to distressing and absurd degrees. In the more conservative parts of India, an elderly woman in trousers would almost certainly arouse sniggers and, from the men, vulgar (I use the word in preference to *lewd* or *smutty* since it could exclude these overtones but be in bad taste even without them) comments. Similarly, girls who do not conform to traditional modes of dress are termed 'loose' and 'immoral'. A slight degree of flamboyance in dress or behaviour is interpreted as an unambiguous come-hither signal. The sexual harassment of college-going girls is routinely justified on the grounds that they 'ask for it' by dressing provocatively.

The onus is clearly on the girl alone. The barbaric behaviour of boys who may be her school or college mates, or of other men known and unknown, is seen as having been triggered off by her alleged lack of morals. Worse, it is frequently argued that boys/men are *naturally* libidinous and therefore not to be held accountable for their sexual misdemeanours if girls/women set themselves out to deliberately provoke them.

It may be argued that the association of morals with modes of dress is common to all societies, and that sexual harassment is not confined to our context. Every newspaper abroad has some reference or the other to such harassment. Thirteen-year-old Tawnya Brawdy of California had to put up with about fifteen to thirty boys chanting rude epithets like 'moo moo' and 'big tits', flipping up her skirt and pawing her several times during the day at school. This affected her grades, but her mother's complaints to officials met with the usual 'boys will be boys' response. Eventually, the family had to file a complaint with the Office of Civil Rights in Santa Rosa, California. This was in January 1989. The school district was charged with culpability in the creation of a 'hostile environment' and agreed to an out of court settlement of $20,000. Yet, as Tawnya's mother maintained, this did not compensate the mental damage caused by these acts and the unpleasant publicity that resulted out of the whole event ('Womanews', *The Chicago Tribune,* 8 November 1992, Section 6).

In the same report Nan Stein, who directed a Massachusetts study on teen sexual harassment, points out that schools generally provide a training ground for violence against women because boys are allowed to get away with the idea that sexual harassment is all in the game. A mother whose daughter, like Tawnya, had to file a case for sexual harassment against her school, believes that such harassment has little to do with sexual attraction and a great deal to with power.

Nearly everyone was agreed that such instances needed to be handled *openly*, and that those who were harassed should be encouraged to talk about the experience so that it could be stopped. There were moves afoot to pressurize schools into displaying notices which would prominently and unambiguously list what could be construed as sexual harassment.

The point here is that while sexual harassment is common enough, the degree to which one has access to forms of redressal varies. It is virtually non-existent in our society. Moreover, such references to the global prevalence of the phenomenon are liable to be dangerously manipulated because they provide an easy escape-route and can be used to rationalize the presence of similar situations in India. It should not be overlooked that in India, in spite of the growing militancy among groups of women and the resultant seriousness with which women's issues are being studied at various levels, very little attention is given to the real, nightmarish harassment most girls face in their growing years.

Most often, this goes unnoticed because girls are conditioned into suppressing the fact that these things happen to them out of a sense of futility, fear and shame. In the school I went to, we could not possibly have hoped for sympathy as regards these experiences even if we had chosen to talk about them. We were taught to think of our growing bodies as shameful and told to conceal any signs of natural female curves. We put up with the most humiliating physical assaults on our bodies because we were too scared of being blamed for having invited them.

Adolescent and teenage girls in India even today instinctively flinch when they see a group of boys approaching them from the opposite direction. They grow expert at holding their books, bags, anything they have with them, as shields to protect themselves from groping fingers that, in passing, could either tickle or sadistically squeeze hard. A school-friend of mine once spent a miserable evening with her family at the cinema, silently suffering the man in front who caressed her legs till her father saw him doing it, roared the hall down and made the ushers eject him. Even now, so may women I know protest their inability to cope with men who stand close behind them on crowded buses and rub their penises against them in rhythm to the jerky motion of the bus. The way one is dressed never has or had anything to do with this ongoing process of socially sanctioned molestation. It is merely an expression of what boys/men have been allowed to get away with.

I grew up at a time when the popular Hindi cinema used to show the hero placing the lady of his dreams on his bicycle and riding off with her into the hazy distance, singing long, sentimental love-songs. These heroes were languid young men, with wavy locks and dreamy faces. They represented male supremacy in a definite if muted way, but they were also imbued with an old-world courtesy. Their present-day counterparts are tough, no-nonsense men. Some of them lack the prescribed macho build. They make up for it by swaggering here and there, handkerchiefs around their necks, surrounded by people who are allegedly college-boys but look more like local hoods. They grab the girl they want to score a point over, someone who is usually immune to their charms and has to be broken in, generally in the crudest manner imaginable. She is carried/shoved/thrown into the centre of macho settings—wrestling rings, dockyards, etc. Here she is forcibly kissed by the hero while his companions hoot in glee. Worse, the girl eventually surrenders and even falls in love.

One might argue that both depictions are questionable. A rigid feminist view may even condemn the earlier chivalric hero as a mere eyewash for the grimmer reality of female oppression. Yet, there is a qualitative difference in the world-view which creates the two types. The former was admittedly a romanticized depiction, a media-attempt to create an idealized imaging of the male-female relationship which may have had little or no contact with the seamier reality. But, if the medium is the message, and in India it is overpoweringly so, the cinema at least posited a different perspective, one which may have influenced its viewers in a harmless, if limited way. The hold of the cinema and its bizarre world on the national psyche in India is all too obvious, and increasingly so.

This is why the present-day alternative which the cinema offers is questionable in every respect. It not only degrades women and girls, but poohs-poohs the possibility that a girl could actually resist the dubious sex-appeal of a Rambo clone and get away with it. It glorifies violence and suggests that the tough, amoral approach always works with women. The medium is still the message, but while the essential reality may not have changed all that much, the 'hero's' attitude to it has. He inspires a growing generation to prove its 'manliness' in much the same way. He eventually makes possible a social environment wherein a girl is raped by her friends in college, another one brutally murdered by her rejected lover during a public examination, a third burnt alive because she dared tell her brother about some boys who had molested her, and so on.

If the sexual harassment of adolescent/young girls is more or less global, as the case of Tawnya Brawdy showed, it is also true that the girl-child in countries like India is far more ill-equipped to handle it. Her cultural conditioning keeps her ignorant of the naturalness of the relationship between the sexes. She continues rooted in fear, shame, revulsion and guilt. She is schooled into believing that her relationship with the male sex will have to be censored and shaped by her elders, i.e., that it ought not to develop in a spontaneous or impulsive way. As a result, the question of discussing any experience of sexual harassment does not arise. An unpleasant encounter is usually suppressed, because these subjects are not open to frank discussion. Moreover, she is ashamed, even scared, that she will be accused of having provoked the incident.

Our persistent refusal to acknowledge the large-scale prevalence of child abuse and incest is a case in point. At a seminar on women's discourse held in Mysore in January 1994, several male participants dismissed the relevance of the theme of child abuse. A moving exposé of the subject by a foreign participant, herself a victim of child abuse, was categorized as a Western aberration by these men, who spoke glowingly of the traditional Indian love for children.

The fact is that the joint family could promote the sexual abuse of girls, especially under the sorts of pressures in which present-day households operate. In more straitened circumstances, the abuse of girl-children is neither unknown nor infrequent. Fathers are known to rape their children, often with the acquiescence of the mother who is too afraid to protest. Mothers have even been known to keep silent out of a mistaken notion of preserving the family *izzat*. In a recent verdict, the Bombay High Court actually reduced the sentence awarded to a father-rapist on the grounds that his economic circumstances (he was a pavement-dweller) could have resulted in pressures which, in turn, could have pushed him into raping his own daughter.

If the experience is at all revealed by the girl, it becomes a convenient tool of argument to rationalize the need to keep her in purdah. A girl in the West may interact with a large number of her peers of either sex and eventually apprehend her situation at an intellectual level. This could equip her with a set of defences/principles/choices even if it does not necessarily result in a 'happy' solution (i.e. a balanced emotional relationship with an understanding male). The Indian girl, on the other hand, is generally not offered any alternatives. Denial of bodily freedom is only one aspect of a no-exit syndrome.

Sexism is even now perpetuated through the school curricula which make a clear distinction between what boys and girls should 'learn' in a non-pedagogic sense. Boys are exempted from even basic needlework and cookery and, worse, are actually encouraged to dismiss this and other household chores as 'girls' work'. Handicraft classes in most girls' schools focus on worthless trivia. The girl is taught to fashion these in the manner of, for instance, Victorian society which saw women's spare time as best suited to idle pastimes and the creation of useless monstrosities. A girl who resists such 'education' may be penalized, humiliated, and is usually denied a grade or a rank.

School-lessons emphasize type-roles. Children are taught to think of an ideal family as one in which the father works, the mother keeps home, and the children express stereotypical ambitions when not showing their love for their parents in impossibly unreal ways. A popular kindergarten playtime chant indicates something of the way in which even a seeming movement away from this conventional world-view only serves to absorb accepted categories, by grouping the women into extensional roles while the men are identified with the competitive or aggressive ones. The children chanting the words assert that their fathers are doctors, their mothers teachers, their sisters dancers and their brothers boxers!

This is not a very far step ahead from the kindergarten chant *I* learnt, in which little girls were seen as made of sugar and spice and all things nice, while little boys were made of frogs and snails and puppy dogs' tails. The uncritical manner in which we let this rhyme sink into our minds coloured our tacit assumption that little girls had to be sugary and spicy, sweet-smelling and cuddly, while little boys could, by some mysterious sanction, be otherwise. As we grew older, we were exposed to other forms of subtle discrimination—the sorts of games we could play, for instance. Boys had slings, football and cricket, whereas we girls had bhātuklīs.[30]

No girl I can remember from my childhood was ever given a meccano-set for her birthday, while at least one boy who wanted a doll was unceremoniously told not to be like a girl. When I was about eight, a popular Marathi song clearly testified that the sugar-and-spice syndrome was a universal one even if the rhyme was English. The words of the song, sung in a high-pitched, little-girlish manner, went like this: *Gŏrī-gŏrī-paan, phulaa saarkhee chaan, Dādā malaa eka vahini aaṇ*. These lines, in which the little girl exhorts her elder brother to bring home a sister-in-law who is very fair and as pretty as a flower, set the tone for the rest of the song. It develops into a long catalogue of the younger sister's preferences as regards the physical attributes of a would-be sister-in-law, all of which repeat the stereotypical images of femininity. What is revealing, moreover, is the fact that a *young girl* sings these lines, for it indicates how notions of what Greer called *the eternal feminine* are insidiously transmitted through popular culture and become unquestioned norms.

The treatment of the girl-child in Indian literature reaffirms the predominance of the Indian world-view. Even where the literature is in revolt against such traditionalism, the critique assumes the undisputed commonness of beliefs and attitudes towards girls. Some of the references made in this chapter to Tagore show how his girl-children are perceived as girl-women. This category is found in the literature of virtually every Indian language. What is more, it takes shape from the social context which, even today, has hardly changed.

In spite of superficial advances, the conventional image of the Indian girl-child is that of a metaphoriacal Janus: two-faced, literally speaking, little girl as sugar-and-spice on the one hand and little girl-woman as general dogsbody on the other. These are the faces of advertising (the 'I-love-you-Rasna' type alongside the girl who is slapped by her mother in the government message referred to earlier); of the cinema (Durga in Satyajit Ray's *Pather Panchali*); and of newspaper reports. But there are also the stories which never make the headlines. A female relative, it is rumoured, turned her face from her second-born, a daughter like the first, with a weary 'Throw her away'. She bears out the depiction of the hysterical mother in Shashi Deshpande's *The Dark Holds No Terrors* (Penguin India, 1990), who never forgave her daughter for being alive when her brother drowned. Years later, the protagonist can still remember the traumatizing effect of the mother's outburst, and of 'the words that followed me for days, months; years, all my life. *You killed him. Why didn't you die? Why are you alive, when he's dead?*' (p. 191).

In my introductory chapter, I had touched on the theme of jāti in a gender-related context, and commented on the way in which gender had become the greatest equalizer at least for the women in India. The girl-child's caste, stamped while she is still unborn, brands her for life. She goes through girlhood, preparing for *the* big event in her life: *marriage*. She may have her marriage arranged while she is still a little girl. She may or may not be married off before puberty, but till she is she lives in a sort of limbo, where every freedom and joy is measured by its being a temporary one. Unmarried, she will forever be an enigma. Married, she enters a new phase of bondage. The implications of this phase form the subject of the next chapter.

Chapter 3

Vivāha
(Marriage)

VIEWPOINT
(A Modern Indian Ballad)

Bring out the silver and polish the brass
Brush off the cobwebs and clean all the glass
Unlock the pantry, lay out the food
Keep away grandma, her manners are crude.

We've got a daughter we're willing to sell
His is the bargain, the profit as well:
He's coming to see for himself, so he said,
How she and our money would look in his bed.

Our daughter's a graduate, he's no cause to moan
She's a well-brought-up girl with no mind of her own
She speaks English well, has a fair pretty face,
And is five foot four inches by Lord Bhagwan's grace.

Of course she'll be happy, I'll tell you that flat:
She'll have her own home, produce brat after brat,

Forget all her youth as she spins out her life
In waddling behind him, a good Indian wife.

And she'll long to have sons: they're boons from above
Take it from me that they're proof of God's love
And when all her daughters are suitably grown,
She'll marry them off as we've done our own.

Vrinda Nabar

According to scholars like P. V. Kane, marriage is the most important of all saṁskāras[1] and the available evidence would indicate that the institution of marriage existed in our society from the earliest times (*History of the Dharmaśāstra,* Vol. II, Chapter IX, p. 427). It is undoubtedly *the* central priority of our social life today, and would seem to be the end towards which all girls are conditioned to believe they should be moving. Undoubtedly again, for most of them marriage amounts to what Ursula in D. H. Lawrence's novel *Women in Love* flippantly described it as: 'the end of experience' (Penguin, 1967, p.7).

The certainty Kane displays as regards the prevalence of the institution of marriage is challenged by others. In *Dāsa-Śūdra Slavery*: *Studies in the Origins of Indian Slavery and Feudalism and Their Philosophies* (Allied Publishers, New Delhi, 1982), Sharad Patil maintains that 'the first "dharma" of mankind was ritual promiscuous copulation' (p. 126), and refers us to Irawati Karve's *Kinship Organization in India* for a more detailed discussion on this issue.

Patil's argument is of obvious interest in a study of changing social structures. For instance, he discusses Kane's distinction between *matriarchal polyandry* ('where a woman forms simultaneous alliances with two or more men who are not necessarily relations of each other and therefore succession is traced through the female') and *fraternal polyandry* ('where a woman becomes the wife of several brothers') and concludes that fraternal polyandry was 'the first step made by maternal polyandry in the direction of patriarchy' (p. 129).

It is significant that these details are not central to the present-day Indian outlook which rarely goes beyond the Brahminical system of laws for its rationalization of social practices which, in turn, have nothing to do today with being a Brahmin or otherwise. If one is to challenge the basis for some of the fundamental codes about women, one would have to willy-nilly focus on the Śāstras and on the saṁskāras derived from them. Though most Indians would not be aware of or interested in the innumerable sources which govern present-day strictures in codes of conduct, it is safe to claim that such strictures have influenced our collective unconscious through the ages to a substantial extent. While the average Hindu may be ignorant of the Śāstras in all their variety, it is because of their insidious hold on his psyche that the urge to marry is seen as such a social imperative.

The traditional Hindu world-view saw a man's life as defined by four distinct phases and the roles he was required to play in each. The second of these four stages was the gṛhasthāśrama in which he played the role of the householder. The *Ṛgveda* (X.85.36) asserts that it was *marriage* which enabled a man to become a householder. Marriage, in turn, made it possible for him to perform sacrifices to the gods and to procreate *sons*. Moreover, certain rituals could only be performed in the state of matrimony. It is significant that the aim of marriage is commonly seen as the procreation of *sons*, not *daughters*. The sons would inherit the right to perform the same sacrifices in a self-perpetuating manner, hence the need to bear them. It apparently did not seem to occur to anyone that if there were no daughters there could be no sons, since there would be no women to bear them.

Kane maintains that the references to a time in history when marriage did not exist are few and far between. What is more, according to the orthodox view (which he clearly represents), most of them would seem to describe such a period as one of unrestrained wantonness among women: while Vedic sources make no reference to a promiscuous or unregulated life-style at any point in time, the *Mahābhārata* has Pāṇḍu tell his queen Kunti that women in earlier times were sexually licentious (Vol.II, p. 427). Kane would, however, prefer to discount even these references, on the somewhat tenuous ground that 'The theory of an original state of promiscuity once advanced by several sociologists has now ceased to be respectable' (p. 428). The possibility of such 'promiscuity' having another, rational and utilitarian purpose, is obviously not part of this mode of thinking.

The anthropological argument of female centrality in the earliest agricultural societies clearly points to the role of woman as life-giver and, therefore, fertility-symbol. The presence of 'ritual sexual promiscuity and polyandry' (Sharad Patil, p. 103) among primitive societies all over the world had a great deal to do with this perception of woman as a fertility-symbol rather than with her alleged lack of sexual restraint. The later depiction of her as in need of strict control coincides with the spread of the patriarchal code and is clearly intended to rationalize the need to straitjacket women.

It is a curious fact common to all 'recent' cultures that women have been consistently portrayed as wanton, sinful, treacherous, and filled with sensual lust. At the same time, all evidence of the recorded history of these cultures points to their being constrained and enslaved at virtually every step. In *The First Sex,* Elizabeth Gould Davis analyses the Judaeo-Christian ambivalence towards women in the context of the patriarchal revolution, and argues that ancient myths were often altered to emphasize the patriarchal world-order. Among these is the one most crucial to the Judaeo-Christian world-view, viz. 'Genesis'.

Davis sees the story as a bowdlerization of an ancient legend, that of the goddess Tiamat, the creator of the universe in the Sumerian civilization. In the *Enuma Elish*, the creation of the world is described thus: 'In the beginning Tiamat brought forth the heaven and the earth . . . Tiamat, the mother of the gods, creator of all.' These lines became 'In the beginning *God* created the heavens and the earth . . .' (pp. 141–2). According to Davis, even the story of Adam and Eve is transformed: in one account she is created at the same time as Adam, while in another 'God creates Adam, then the animals, and finally, as an after-thought, makes woman out of Adam's rib!' (p. 142).

Davis also seeks to interpret the Hindu god Rāma as 'the dissident Aryan . . . [who] converted India from gynarchy and goddess worship before our era.' Unable to overthrow the power and authority of women in his native land—somewhere in Anatolia or Southern Europe—he left his country and eventually found his way into India (p. 134).

While the soundness of *this* thesis is best left to experts (the Rāma-Sītā dialectic and its hold on the Indian psyche is discussed later in this chapter), it is worth noting that a more or less similar point is made by Rupert Sheldrake in *The Rebirth of Nature: The Greening of Science and God* (Bantam Books, 1991). Sheldrake maintains that early agricultural societies in Europe lived peacefully for several thousand years. They worshipped goddesses and made superb ceramics rather than weapons. Somewhere between 4000 and 3500 BC, however, this pattern was changed by invading tribes and the old goddesses were reduced to becoming the 'wives, daughters, and consorts' of the new warrior-gods. This was the beginning of patriarchy and male-domination. Sheldrake argues that a similar transformation took place in India with the advent of the Aryans (pp. 17–18).

In the *Anthology of Sacred Texts By and About Women* (New York, Pandora, Harper Collins, 1993) editor Serinity Young, while deploring the exclusion of women from most 'significant and meaningful studies of religion' (p.ix), also observes that the concept of male divinity and the male dominance of religious roles are both fairly recent developments. Young also holds that the evidence of recent scholarship would suggest that it was women who were the repositories of religious knowledge and expertise (p.xi).

What is interesting both in the evidence of an earlier gynocentric stage in human history and in its supersession by the androcentric one of patriarchy is the seeming contradiction between the present-day patriarchal insistence on women as *naturally monogamous* and men as *natural philanderers* and the perspective (also a patriarchal one) on the alleged promiscuity of untethered women.

In the Hindu scheme of things, the several terms ūsed to denote the saṁskāras of marriage underline the discrimination that is implicit in the very idea of marriage. Udvāha signifies that a girl is taken away from the home into which she was born (i.e. her father's home); vivāha implies that a girl is taken away for a specific purpose (clear in this instance), and in a special way; pāṇigrahaṇa means the taking of the girl's hand, a conjoining as it were of man and woman in marriage.[2] In all these, as in the other saṁskāras, the girl/woman is seen as the passive principle, the male as the active one. It is he who executes the act, or leads it, she who is affected by the act and/or follows him.

The Śāstras would seem to emphasize the dialectics of marriage, and indeed this dialectics forms the very basis of the Hindu world-view. Rāma is inconceivable without Sītā, Kṛṣṇa without Rādhā, Satyavāna without Sāvitrī, and so on. Heinrich Zimmer has commented on the importance of this dialectical perspective in the Hindu tradition and has pointed out that the lingam (symbolizing male creative energy) and the yoni (the symbol of female creative energy) are frequently combined in such a way that the latter forms the base of the image, the former rising from its centre (*Myths and Symbols in Indian Art and Civilization*, ed. Joseph Campbell,

Pantheon Books, Bollingen Series VI, 4th printing, 1963, p. 127).

'Children, the fulfilment of duties, obedience, and the ultimate sexual pleasure depend upon a wife, and so heaven, for oneself and one's ancestors.' (*Manu*, *9.28*, p. 200). The śāstras are by and large agreed on the fact that the wife is necessary for a man's fulfilment. She is the ardhāngini, and when a man 'secures a wife, he gets progeny and then he becomes complete.' (*Sat.Br.* V.2.10, Kane, p. 428).

Yet, we have already seen that the requirements of the ideal bride far outweigh those of the ideal bridegroom, and the extent to which these mould popular consciousness may be seen in the 'matrimonial columns' of our leading dailies, where the qualities desired in a bride are elaborated on in great detail. The same method is at work in the humiliating exhibition which is generally made of a 'marriageable' daughter: the proposal, the visit by the young man and his family to inspect her en route to inspecting several other girls, the display of all her talents (cookery, music, flower-arrangements, embroidery) in the space of an hour, the questions to which she is subjected, and the final acceptance or rejection of her as marriage-material, all add up to the same thing qualitatively.

As already seen in Chapter 2, strictures about inter-varṇa marriages are clearly weighted in the favour of men. By denying women the same degree of flexibility, their less-than-equal status as well as their absence of freedom to act according to their desires in matters of marriage were unequivocally stated. The fact that, theoretically at least, a man of a higher varṇa could marry a woman of a lower varṇa while a woman of a higher varṇa was denied the same freedom suggests that the man was seen as bringing his wife to his level, whether high or low. In other words, with marriage a woman's whole being took on the characteristics of her husband's. 'When a woman is joined with a husband in accordance with the rules, she takes on the same qualities that he has, just like a river flowing down into the ocean' (Manu, 9.22, p.199).

Manu's statement, quoted earlier, about a wife being important for the happiness of a man and his ancestors (9.28) follows on a series of negative pronouncements which, taken together, reaffirm his basic theme about women being unfit for independence (9.3). Men are even instructed to *make* women dependent on them (9.2). This duty passes from *father* to *son* (9.4). So essential does this seem in his scheme of things, that men are warned that failure to do so attaches 'blame' to them, should anything go amiss (9.4). Unguarded women 'bring sorrow upon both families' (9.5). Women are easily corrupted and need therefore to be kept occupied (9.10–11). Their sexual instincts are uncontrollable and they are naturally promiscuous (9.14–16). In conclusion, this is why they are denied access to the performance—in or by themselves—of Vedic rituals. 'For women, who have no virile strength and no Vedic verses, are falsehood, this is well established' (9.18) (*Manu,* pp. 197–98).

Muslim reformist thinkers have also commented on the fact that though Islamic history has deviated considerably from Islamic norms, there is enough evidence in the Koran to suggest that women were seen as inherently inferior. In his article on 'The Status of Women in Islam: A Modernist Interpretation', Fazlur Rahman sees such evidence as implying 'socioeconomic' as against 'essential or inherent' inequality (*Separate Worlds: Studies of Purdah in South Asia*, ed. Hanna Papanek and Gail Minault, New Delhi, Chanakya Publications, 1982, p. 294). However, as his own quotations exemplify, it is doubtful whether the two are mutually exclusive. 'For them (i.e. women) there are rights (against men) that are exactly commensurate with their obligations (towards them), but men are one degree higher than women' (2:228, p. 294).

Rahman maintains that this statement applies to the social not the religious, sphere. It is questionable, however, whether one can distinguish the two spheres so absolutely. I would see them as interacting and influencing one another. To explain this statement from the Koran, Rahman quotes from 4:34, which states that men are 'managers over' women in the way that some human beings are naturally better than others in certain respects. Men also spend their wealth on their women. Therefore, good women are faithful to their husbands in their absence and guard what is the husband's as God meant them to. Women who are wayward should be rebuked, then left alone in their beds, and finally beaten (p. 294).

Rahman interprets the many occurrences of the phrase 'excelling others' in the Koran to mean that some humans perform better than others and discounts any possible implications of inherent inequality. He also maintains that the phrase cannot be seen as connoting gender inequality. He concludes therefore that if the Koran sees men as better managers and controllers, it is because male experience has made man better-equipped to handle certain matters. Though Rahman grants that these conditions are not unchangeable (he has to since he has also argued against their being inherent), he remains doubtful as to 'whether women should ask or be allowed to do any and all jobs that men do' (p. 295).

There are several assumptions implicit in the statements from which Rahman quotes, assumptions which he does not analyse closely enough. For instance, in the passage just referred to, individual excellence in allied with gender excellence: men are seen as superior to women because 'some of humankind excel others'. This is a definitive statement about *gender* potential and discriminates between male and female abilities, regarding the first as implicitly superior. Rahman's line of reasoning underscores the discrimination: an observation about the differing capabilities of individuals is arbitrarily used to explain an alleged gender superiority without any convincing rational basis to the stand taken.

It is further affirmed that God has assigned duties of subservience and devotion to women, and that those who fall in line are 'good' women. The value judgement attached to this statement is clearly a warning to would-be transgressors—they are, by implication, not 'good' women. Rahman also appears singularly unmoved by the permission granted to husbands to beat their wives. Though he qualifies this statement by maintaining that they were to beat them 'without causing injury' (p. 295), what is really questionable here is the sanction given to a husband to beat a wife who is 'wayward', and this sanction Rahman leaves well alone.

I draw attention to Rahman's tacit acceptance of these injunctions (which he does rationalize in a liberal sort of way) because I find it distressing that a so-called 'post-modernist' view should display the same kind of limited questioning which would characterize a more traditional approach. Both appear to use the texts/scriptures to rationalize a social condition without examining whether, the conditions are in themselves justified. Both, again, do not examine whether the assumptions made are verifiable in a non-subjective, non-faith context, as well as the dangers implicit in these assumptions.

Rahman's argument, which is fundamentally an enlightened one, illustrates how a society's canonical texts can and do mould popular consciousness. This can create patterns of thought as well as attitudes which are irretrievably rooted in a hypothesis whose fallibility is never questioned or seen as faulty. Thus, while Rahman admits that traditional customs and attitudes in Muslim societies need to be changed becausc of the gross abuse of a woman's dependence on man, he himself is clearly unable to perceive the fundamental assumptions about women as being flawed. A similar limitation in several so-called liberal commentators has resulted in the continued exploitation and abuse of women. This is not surprising when the popular consciousness through the ages, in different cultures and religions, has come to apprehend women as essentially unreliable and fickle. Understandably, therefore, the primary male-female relationship which in all traditional societies constitutes marriage, has been seen as a justifiably unequal one.

Since marriage was seen as necessary for the creation of progeny and the perpetuation of one's line, it is hardly surprising that so much emphasis was laid on the woman's role as child-bearer. 'Once the relevance of coition to childbirth was recognized by men as well as by women, the status of men gradually improved' (*The First Sex,* p. 121). Manu unambiguously defines the terms of the equation which constitutes the male-female bonding in marriage: 'the revealed canon is divided in two about who the "husband" is: some say that he is the begetter, others that he is *the one who owns the field*' (9.32, pp. 200–1).

It is clear from *Manu* (9.33) that the woman is traditionally regarded as the field, the man as the seed. Nor is there room for any doubt as to the respective power of each. The seed is given priority over the womb, for 'the offspring of all living beings are marked by the mark of the seed'. If the seed is sown in the ground at the right time, only the fruit of that seed springs from the soil, and in doing so it reflects none of the qualities of the womb (earth) from which it has sprung (9.35–37, pp. 201).

Present-day genetics would no doubt disprove this world-view. Genetics notwithstanding, however, the manifestation of social attitudes in matters such as child-bearing show how even conservatism can conveniently look the other way when patriarchal well-being is threatened. Manu's strictures, if accepted in toto, would mean that the onus of what was procreated rested with the man, but even the most rigid traditionalist would prefer to ignore *this* ruling while supporting most others. Social experience clearly points to the fact that all blame for alleged inadequacies in the process of childbirth, from actual conception to the sex of the child and its safe delivery is attributed to the feckless wife.

Several writers have handled this theme. In Nayantara Sahgal's novel *Mistaken Identity* (William Heinemann, London, 1988), the protagonist Bhushan's mother is dragged off on a series of pilgrimages to propitiate the gods so that they may bless her womb with a male foetus. It is usually the woman who is termed barren, not the male who admits that he could be sterile. The inability to conceive as well as the inability to conceive a *male* child are viewed as failures for which the woman is generally held accountable. From what one hears and reads, most men are reluctant to test themselves for possible sexual inadequacies, not so much through fear as through a sense of outrage at the implication that their virility is being questioned. Stories of women being abandoned by their husbands for their alleged inability to bear a son are not uncommon.

Ironically, therefore, most males would prefer to overlook Manu's inconvenient pronouncement about their culpability in matters related to eugenics. However, they would unquestioningly accept another statement contained in the same section, viz. that they own their wives' bodies like fields which they plough and sow in.

Images of ownership are of course universal and originate in partriarchal feudalism. Lévi-Strauss has commented on the matrimonial vocabulary of Great Russia, where the groom was called the 'merchant' and the bride the 'merchandise' in order to draw attention to the all-pervading likening of women to commodities (*The Elementary Structures of Kinship*, Boston, Beacon Press, 1969, p.36). Our own mythologies and socio-cultural traditions, along with our social and political history, are, however, full of instances and examples which glorify and romanticize this aspect of feudal gender-ownership.

The most accessible example of such romanticizing is undoubtedly to be found in the *Rāmāyaṇa,* in the figure of Sītā. There have been women, goddesses and apsarās before

Sītā in our cultural past. Sītā however remains one of the most accessible among Indian legends and is representative, to the contemporary Indian mind as a whole, of all that is desired of and desirable in a woman. Sītā marries Rāma, prince of Ayodhyā and avatār of Viṣṇu. Soon after the marriage, Rāma is banished to the forest for fourteen years because of the jealous whim of Kaikeyī, one of his father Daśaratha's consorts.

It is worth noting that while in all popular versions of the *Rāmāyaṇa* Kaikeyī is projected as a scheming, calculating woman, driven only by blind ambition to see her son Bharata rule Ayodhyā, Patil draws our attention to the sociological basis for Daśaratha's action. He says that whereas in a matriarchy the woman naturally headed the clan, phatry and tribe, a fraternal clan marriage between two different tribes involved a condition called 'rājya-śulkā'. This meant that the offspring of no other wife could become the king. It was on this condition that Kaikeyī was given to Daśaratha by her father, the king of the Kekayas (p. 131).

Sītā willingly shares Rāma's exile. She gives up a life of luxury and opulence for the hardships of the jungle. In spite of these glimpses of her overwhelming devotion to her husband, her *female caprice* makes her send Rāma to hunt down a golden deer whose glitter, it is implied, naturally attracts her covetous female soul. She is unable to perceive that the deer is actually a demon, viz. Māriccha, maternal uncle of the demon-king Rāvaṇa.[3] It need hardly be emphasized that Satan had reportedly beguiled Eve in a more or less similar fashion, and that examples of this kind reassert the patriarchal (prejudiced) conviction as regards the fickleness of womankind!

Having committed this act of folly, Sītā does worse. When the defeated Māriccha cries out in Rāma's voice, she fails to see the deception. She attempts to contravene Rāma's orders, and insists that her brother-in-law Lakṣmaṇa go to his help. Lakṣmaṇa is reluctant to disobey his older brother since that would also mean leaving Sītā unprotected. At this, Sītā even taunts him, accusing him of having evil designs on her. In this way she virtually goads him into leaving her alone. When Lakṣmaṇa goes to assist Rāma, he does so on one condition: that Sītā would on no account cross the line of safety he draws in the courtyard. So long as Sītā remained on the right side of the Lakṣmaṇa-rekhā,[4] she would be safe.

The Lakṣmaṇa-rekhā is rich with symbolic overtones. On the literal, narrative level, Sītā of course crosses over it with characteristic female thoughtlessness in spite of Lakṣmaṇa's injunctions. It is hardly relevant to the discussion to point out that she does so in order to serve a wandering bhikshu in keeping with Indian traditions of hospitality. For the bhikshu is none other than Rāvaṇa in disguise, and it is more convenient to imply that this is one more instance of Sītā's short-sightedness. She is unceremoniously abducted by Rāvaṇa who carries her off to his kingdom.

However, it is also crucial to realize that the Lakṣmaṇa-rekhā could in fact be viewed as a form of constraint, a line which Sītā, *as woman,* had no right to cross over. It was a boundary drawn by a male, who had been deputed by another male to guard Sītā the female. When Sītā failed to obey the male dictate and crossed the line, she saw why it was necessary to remain confined to where the male world wanted her to stay. Even Rāvaṇa could be seen as embodying the male principle. In fact he could on one level be interpreted as representing the hostile male which resents her crossing over the decreed boundaries and therefore carries her off.

The Lakṣmaṇa-rekhā is so bound up with the complex tangle between religion and mythology in the Hindu mind that it has rarely been perceived by the popular mind as anything more than what the epic represents it as: a line drawn to guard Sītā. Such a perception fits in naturally with the world-view of the Śāstras, viz. that women were best guarded night and day. This view of the rekhā is given a clever twist in a Marathi poem entitled 'Lakṣmaṇa-rekhā' by Padma Gole,[5] part of which I translate below:

Lakṣmaṇa drew but one line
in front of Sītā.
She crossed over it—
the result was the *Rāmāyaṇa*.
We face Lakṣmaṇa-rekhās
on all sides:
they have to be crossed,
the Rāvaṇas confronted.

Sītā's abduction would support Manu's insistence on the absolute need to guard women. It hardly seems worth the effort to point out that things would never have come to this stage if Lakṣmaṇa had not spurned the amorous advances of Rāvaṇa's sister Śūrpaṇakha. Sītā's abduction was incidental to Rāvaṇa's determination to avenge his sister's humiliation.

Finding Sītā gone, Rāma moves every physical and supernatural force imaginable to bring her back. Ironically, though, having rescued her, he feels that honour demands that she prove that she had remained chaste during the time she spent in Rāvaṇa's palace.

The fact that Sītā was forcefully carried off to avenge Lakṣmaṇa's repudiation of Rāvaṇa's sister Śūrpanakha, or that she was unjustly kept a prisoner seems, surprisingly, of no significance at this moment. It does not appear to occur to Rāma that even if Sītā had been sexually abused, it would have been an act of force for which she could not be held accountable.

Sītā's having had to *prove* her chastity is qualitatively not very different from the manner in which Mathura[6] and the other contemporary women abducted by force and/or sexually abused are required to prove that the sexual act was rape and not one by mutual consent. Sītā passes the test, the agni-parīkṣā, and comes out of this literal ordeal by fire unsigned: an easier proposition in some ways than the burden of proof which contemporary society demands from its women, since Agni (the fire-god) himself puts out the flames and intervenes forcefully on her behalf.

It is revealing enough that, throughout Indian history Sītā's agni-parīkṣā has been glorified rather than condemned. What is even worse however is that some time later Rāma, horrified to learn that his kingdom is abuzz with lurid stories of Sītā's conduct in Lankā, actually feels obliged, as an ideal king, to exile her to the forest even though she is pregnant. Moreover, this is an act for which he has been immortalized in the Indian consciousness as a role-model for all those in power—a ruler who placed the ethics of public life above personal gratification. Rāma's name has cropped up over and over again in recent political debates in India: he was seen as being in glorious contrast to the self-serving nepotism and greed of several contemporary politicians.

In the process however, Sītā was clearly seen as dispensable. Scholarship and popular response have hardly ever viewed these two episodes concerning Sītā critically or used them to show Rāma in a poor light. On the contrary Sītā's *blamelessness* was consistently slurred over. In a recent soap-opera style rendering of the *Rāmāyaṇa* on television the producer-director, perhaps fearing feminist anger, went so far as to modify the conventional version and show Sītā's exile as being of her own choosing. In other words, not only is Sītā banished, she is shown as *wanting* to be sent away to preserve Rāma's family honour and his peace of mind.

This was a clever ploy, one calculated to appeal to the perceived moral codes of contemporary Indian society. The emphasis on the family *izzat*[7] is one which is basic to the Indian world-outlook even today since the family still remains a very potent force in the social structure. The director defended his modification on the grounds that there were scholarly sources to back him. In opting for this way out, however, he was only adding a further dimension to the popular image of Sītā as a woman who is a glorious martyr. Sītā was merely given contemporary dress. She was turned into what Indian society likes to conceive of as the ideal wife, someone who is willing to sacrifice everything, however unjust the terms of the sacrifice, in order to preserve her husband's family honour and his reputation as ruler.

There is a nasty sequel to the story. Years later, Rāma's twin sons, born in the forest, encounter their father and there is a reunion of sorts which is marred by Rāma's insistence that if Sītā is to return to the palace she should once again undergo the agni-parīkṣā so that the people of Ayodhyā who had not been present at the first one are convinced of her chastity. Sītā (rightly) refuses, and opts to return to the earth's bosom. Daughter of the earth, she is received once again into the mother's womb. Padma Gole's poem, referred to earlier, wryly comments on the very different situation contemporary Sītās face:

Only one thing's missing:
the earth doesn't open up
and take us to its bosom!

Given the compelling power of the Sītā myth, my reading may seem like a distortion of something that is both dear and sacred to the Indian mind. A more down-to-earth story would indicate that I do not exaggerate the insidious and dangerous hold that the Sītā myth has on our popular consciousness. I should also add that as a child I myself was a victim to its hypnotic charm. I saw only Sītā's beauty and 'purity'. Implicit in both were her noble service of her husband and her willingness to submit to his dictates. So enormous was her appeal to me that for a long time I even plagued my parents to change my name to Sītā. It was only much later that I saw, not Sītā *per se* but the popular glorification of her as questionable, exploitative rather than fair. But even this personal response is only marginal to my argument. To extend it, I would have to relate the story of two women, sisters-in-law, whom I shall call Usha and Manisha.

This factual account is also a fairly typical example of what happens in many Indian homes. The degree to which this scenario operates may vary according to other factors, such as class or economic status, but the broad attitudes remain more or less the same. Usha and Manisha are married to two brothers, Appa and Bappa. Appa is the older of the two and has had repeated nervous breakdowns. When these breakdowns occur, he stops going to work and resorts to frequent wife-battering. To keep the family going, Usha works as a domestic in five different households and is willing to perform the most strenuous domestic chores. To date, she has suffered all her husband's beatings and abuse without complaint. To me at any rate, there is something almost masochistic in the manner in which she cowers submissively under her husband's ruthless blows.

Manisha is younger, prettier, and also more rebellious. It was when I questioned her about a black eye that I discovered that she had been the family target for some time. They had alleged that her brother was the cause of Appa's misfortunes, and had even accused him of practising sorcery. Manisha had been repeatedly asked to make him stop harming the family. Her protests that he was innocent had been interpreted as unjustifiable defiance. She was beaten and threatened with other abuse unless she did what the family wanted her to.

What was worse, when I sent for Bappa and told him he should stop hitting his wife, her confiding in me was seen as the worst form of treachery. Usha was held up to her as an example of the ideal wife. *Usha* never defied her husband. *Usha* put up with his beatings and the hardships she had to endure when he didn't work. And, *Usha* never complained or sought redressal: she had preserved the family's *izzat* the way all good Indian wives were supposed to.

The Ushas of my personal experience are perpetuated

in Indian society because of our glorification of all the pativratās in our cultural and mythological past. Contemporary Indian cinema continues to project sickeningly submissive women who are worshipped by their macho sons because of the way in which they had held the family together in spite of drunken, violent husbands. What is questionable here is not the heroism of a woman who struggles against all odds to support those she cares for but the assumption that this is the stuff the good woman/wife/mother is made of: acceptance and endurance beyond all bounds of human patience.

Such idealization of female martyrdom is the cultural legacy of all those impossibly self-denying women of fortitude of whom Sītā is the most popular. Significantly, activists protesting against women-related violence have increasingly targeted the family and the neighbourhood, and insisted on their joint complicity in these acts. A family in which the men openly batter their women should really question whether it has any *izzat* left to speak of. But this is never the case: *izzat* seems to be a female-linked commodity. Its preservation is incumbent upon the woman's behaviour alone, and it appears to be the male prerogative to ensure that she does not jeopardize its delicate balance at any cost.

Draupadī, wife to the five Pāṇḍava brothers in the *Mahābhārata,* and another central symbol in the popular consciousness, has been seen as a more rebellious example of Indian womanhood. But even she is an example of the way in which legend and myth can be absorbed and distorted in the consciousness of a nation. Sharad Patil sees Draupadī's marriage to the Pāṇḍavas as consistent with the story of their mother Kunti whom the sun-god is supposed to have mated with, promising that she would regain her virginity after the union. According to Patil, this gave Kunti the status of a 'tribal mother [who] was a lifelong virgin . . . as a tribal mother Kunti commanded her five sons to enjoy apportioning their alms in the person of Draupadī equitably' (p. 67).

Gayatri Chakravorty Spivak sees Draupadī as providing a singular example of polyandry in marriage, which was not in common practice in India. She becomes even more exceptional because she is placed within a context which is patriarchal and patronymic. The five sons of Pāṇḍu, since they are her 'husbands' and not her 'lovers' are '*legitimately* pluralized' (*Draupadī* by Mahasweta Devi. Translated with a Foreword by Gayatri Chakravorty Spivak. *In Other Worlds: Essays in Cultural Politics,* Routledge, New York, 1987, p. 183.)

What is interesting in the present context is not the possible explanation of the Draupadī legend, but the manner in which the legend has taken hold in popular culture. According to the popular version (by which I mean the story most Indians would know and narrate), Draupadī is wife to the five Pāṇḍavas because of an inadvertent remark made by Kunti in response to a jocular statement of her third son, Arjuna. Arjuna wins Draupadī's hand at her swayaṁvar[8] because of his skill in archery. Since this happens while the Pāṇḍavas are in exile, the princess goes with him to their present home in the jungle. On arrival, Arjuna asks his mother (whose back is to him) to see what the day's alms had yielded and Kunti, without looking around, says as usual, 'Share it among you five brothers.'

So far, so good. But even when the implications of this directive become clear, Kunti does not retract. Nor does anyone, apparently, think of questioning this state of affairs. So Draupadī, willy-nilly, becomes the sexual property of the five brothers. And when they lose everything to their cousins the Kauravas in the fatal game of dice, she is staked as casually as if she is in fact, no more than one of their assets. Worse, it is *she* who is labelled a whore by the victors for having serviced five men, *she* who is sexually humiliated by their attempt to publicly disrobe her, an attempt which is aborted only through the intervention of Lord Kṛṣṇa.

Spivak underscores the manner in which Draupadī's

'legitimate pluralization' (she is a wife with five husbands) becomes the means to 'demonstrate male glory'. Her humiliation triggers off the last, fatal battle. When her eldest husband loses in a game of dice, he stakes her as naturally as everything else he owns. Her peculiar position as the wife of five men is further used by the victors to justify their treatment of her: according to them, since the Scriptures say that a woman can have only one husband, Draupadī is no better than a prostitute and can be dragged into the public assembly even if she is not properly clothed (p. 183).

Yet, the circumstances in which Draupadī is dragged into the assembly are inseparable from the echoes of orthodox taboos which are gender-discriminatory. What is disturbing is that there is no evidence of any reformist purpose in the act. Rather, taboos are flouted to humiliate Draupadī further. She herself reproaches her tormentors, reminding them that she had never been seen in public after the swayaṁvar, and that the Pāṇḍavas had sheltered her from even the touch of the wind in her own house (*The Mahābhārata*, Vol.2. Serenity Young, p. 285).

According to the prevalent code, Draupadī's blatant presence in the assembly was clearly meant to discredit her honour. Moreover, even if her public display is rationalized on the grounds that she was only a prostitute, there is still the other fact, viz. that as a menstruating woman her shame is doubly worse. This shame is uppermost in her mind when Duhśāsana drags her by the hair, but though she appeals to him on these grounds, he tells her that she is now a slave, 'And one lechers with slaves as the fancy befalls!' (*The Mahābhārata*, Vol.2. Young, p. 284).

This exchange, between Draupadī and her husband's cousin Duhśāsana, is followed by her futile outburst in the assembly and climaxes in the attempt to disrobe her. Draupadī's vastṛharaṇ should surely be viewed as one of the most horrendous and shameful events in the cultural history of a nation that still deludes itself about its traditions of protecting a woman's honour and where every constraint put on women is rationalized on those grounds. It is indicative of our mixed-up values and cultural hypocrisy that, when this episode was depicted in a soap-opera style rendering of *The Mahābhārata* on television, what caught the public eye was not the ignominy of Draupadī's experience or its continued relevance to contemporary Indian reality, but rather the sari which Draupadī wore in the episode. A well-known textile company made capital out of announcing that it had manufactured the sari, and that similar ones were being marketed by it in various retail shops. The demand for the Draupadī sari was significant. In this way the trauma of the vastrharaṇ was reduced, in no time at all, to the tawdry glitter of advertising gimmickry and acquisitive greed.

There is a fundamental parity between our perpetuation of mythical stereotypes like Sītā and Draupadī and our present-day reluctance to admit any change that threatens the androcentric, partriarchal set-up. In her poem, 'The Slave', Marathi poet Hira Bansode[9] draws attention to the continuity between myth and reality:

> In that country
> where doors are adorned
> with flowers and mango-leaves,
> the houses decorated
> with lighted lamps,
> in that country
> the woman is still a slave.
> Where Sītā had to pass
> the ordeal by fire
> to prove she was a pativratā,
> Ahilya[10] to sacrifice herself
> to Indra's sexual desire,
> and Draupadī was divided up
> among five men,

the woman of that country
still remains a slave . . .

Bansode also speaks of the crushing force of tradition and of the death of joy and spontaneity brought about by the ritualization of tradition. She concludes that though we celebrate festivals which commemorate spiritual victory, the sad examples listed in her poem serve to assert that a woman's life is filled with oppression and torture.

The list of our myth-heroines is a long one. Sāvitrī battled Yama himself in order to prove her devotion to Satyavāna. When Kāli[11] went on the rampage, her trail of destruction and bloodshed only ceased when Śiva lay in her path. In other words, even the indomitable Kāli had/has her overlord. In recognition of this feudal fact, all the popular idols of the goddess which are on display during the Kāli-puja in Calcutta show this frightening, awe-inspiring goddess sticking out her tongue in a characteristic Indian gesture meant to signify shame and embarrassment. The frightening goddess looks, for all practical purposes, like a very guilty schoolgirl: her sense of shame is contained in the fact that she had inadvertently stepped on Śiva, *her* god and the only force in the universe that could have stopped her onslaught not as god or strength but as her *husband.*

Rajput queens—like Padmini of Chittor who, in defeat, threw herself into the flames along with her royal entourage of women—are singled out for their exemplary fortitude. They are hailed as heroines who preferred to die when their men were defeated/killed rather than to live on as the possible prey of their Islamic conquerors. What is questionable here is not the fortitude implicit in their act but our continued indifference to the fact that they were really exercising a choice without alternatives. It is easily forgotten that while the courage of individual women such as these is what a myth is made up of, the myth itself is, unfortunately, firmly rooted in an ethos which condones the subjugation and sexual abuse of women whether as women or as spoils of war.

No one, apparently, sought to question why these poor women *needed* to die in this ghastly way. There was never any public outcry in any era against the inhumanity of the social mores that reduced a woman to this kind of no-exit situation. The Maratha emperor Shivaji had reportedly warned his officers not to condone the sexual abuse of the enemy's women, but examples such as his are far too sporadic to add up to any meaningful stand. It was more convenient for the most part to glorify such incidents of mass-suicides by conquered women than to censure the reality which made them necessary: the first was a male-serving option while the second called for a more radical change in men's ways of seeing.

Hira Bansode's poem 'Yashodharā' raises certain issues which are an interesting follow-up to this theme. Bansode's poem is about the woman Gautama the Buddha left behind when he set forth to find the path to Nirvāṇa. The story of Gautama, Prince of Kapilavastu, is familiar to every Indian. Sickened by all the visual reminders of human suffering—disease, poverty, old age, death—he left behind his sleeping wife and son and set off to meditate for long years in order to find a way to transcend human suffering. He became the Buddha, the Enlightened One, who was later deified and whose teachings have inspired innumerable people in India and even the Far East.

Bansode compares the Buddha's wife Yashodharā with other significant female figures in our cultural past: Sītā and Draupadī for instance. Rightly or wrongly, their role has been immortalized in cultural history. They have been transformed into symbols, if questionable ones, of Hindu/Indian womanhood, while Yashodharā's fate was as it were sealed the night Gautama left the palace. In the annals of Buddhist/Indian history, Yashodharā plays no memorable part. Only the Buddha is singled out for focus.

What happened to Yashodharā after the prince had

abandoned her is not known—there are sporadic references to her, such as the mention of her giving up their son Rāhul to his father. But, having lost both husband and son, the rest of her life remains a blank. No commentator has questioned her fate, her possible grief, her suffering, the implications to her woman's mind of Gautama's action in renouncing the world. In mutely giving up her son as well, she played the characteristic wifely role of self-obliteration and sacrifice. She was blotted out from all creative memory because of the one act of her husband's which excluded her from his life and deprived hers of all socially perceived meaning.

Yet, Yashodharā's *non-role* is in some senses the end of the road along which our Sītās and Draupadīs have travelled. It is the logical culmination of what these women represent. The *sublimation of oppression,* which Sītā epitomized, gives way to the *desired objective* of such a sublimation: a total surrender of one's very existence if one is a woman. After all, if a woman is merely a field which her husband owns, one may as well argue that women, like fields, have no distinct names or identities.

This assumption is implicit in the global practice of changing a woman's surname after marriage, which passes feudal ownership of the woman from father to husband. In some sections of Indian society, however, it is fairly usual even now for the husband to change his wife's *first* name as well. Nothing could be more symbolic of feudal ownership than this unambiguous assumption that, with marriage, the woman's entire past becomes separate and unconnected with her married life. Moreover, since a name may be seen as conferring a form of identity, a distinctiveness, such a practice implies that it is the husband's prerogative to obliterate his wife's identity, if he so wishes, and to give her a new one of his own choice.

Therefore, if Sītā is idealized as an example of a woman/wife who submits willingly to her husband's priorities, and Draupadī because she gave in to Kunti's bidding and stayed with the Pāṇḍavas in spite of her humiliation, Yashodharā becomes the finished product. Moreover, it should be remembered that Draupadī has never been as unquestioningly accepted and idealized as Sītā. This may be because there is a rebellious streak in her which is absent in Sītā. She is also perhaps less easy to accept in a society where the idea of even a widow being able to want another husband is by and large questioned. Further, her outspoken diatribe against her oppressors is in blatant contrast to Sītā's ready resignation to her fate. She reflects badly on the male world of which she becomes the victim. She gives the lie to our glib insistence on the way we honour our women, since a whole assembly of elders including pitāmahā Bhiṣma[12] sat silent during her vastṛharaṇ. In fact, Draupadī also shames Bhiṣma by upbraiding his complicity in the act and contemptuously dismisses his excuse, viz. that Yudhiṣṭhira[13] had staked her of his own free choice.[14] Yashodharā, however, is testimony to a woman's ultimate fate: she is representative of the submission of a wife to her husband's quest for what will bring *him* fulfilment even if the price *she* pays is self-obliteration.

I have referred in an earlier chapter to the Hindi cinema's projection of stereotyped images. The danger of such cinema lies in the overpowering seductiveness of the medium and the crudely sexist implications of its message. The formula adhered to remains by and large the same though the frills and trappings may vary marginally. At the heart of the story in virtually every film is the moral that love, truth and beauty are all-pervasive, never mind that the rest of the film does its damnedest to suggest otherwise. The girl/woman who hoists the flag of truth et al aloft at the very end is always the archetypal 'Bhāratīya nārī': someone who is self-effacing, self-denying, and given to making a doormat of herself. The pathways by which she arrives at this colourless state are varied and tortuous. She may start out as a flashy 'modern type' college-going teenager or as a brazen hussy flouncing around in the sort of permanent *déshabillé* our celluloid creations favour. Needless to say, there is a heart of gold beneath all the tawdry glitter, but before it can shine forth unblemished the flashiness and brazenness would need to be replaced by our notions of behaviour appropriate to women. There can be no female goodness except in eyes that are modestly lowered, a head that is modestly covered with the sari-pallav, and a voice which is rarely raised above a whisper.

Susan Faludi refers to the insidious propaganda of a film like *Fatal Attraction* which deals with an extra-marital relationship (*Backlash*, pp. 9–10). Faludi's ire is directed at the manner in which the female in this partnership is presented as not merely an unscrupulous seductress but as someone who is amoral, vicious, violent and damaging to all happy marriages. This, of course, includes her own lover's marriage, which *he* would like to continue with once he's had his fill of her. Faludi sees *Fatal Attraction* as part of the 'marriage news' statistics onslaught on feminism, with its message of the single woman as lonely to the point of becoming warped and demented. It is also possible to see films like *Fatal Attraction* as part of the wave of post-AIDS phobia in the West with its insistence on 'safe sex' with a known partner. Both interpretations, however, as indeed the film itself, do come down unfairly on the girl involved. In depicting her as a *femme fatale* gone berserk and helplessly out of control, the man's accountability is conveniently ignored by everyone—the man himself, the audience, and the man's wife.

While our films have yet to achieve this degree of sexual flagrancy, the insidious message of sexism in gender-roles is very present even in films which self-professedly aim at a more 'revolutionary' approach. Sunil Dutt's much-touted *Aag* is one such film, and is the story of a father's determined effort to avenge his daughter's death at the hands of her rapacious husband and in-laws. Allegedly an attack on the atrocities occasioned by the greed for dowry, the protest is successful and the film ends in a way, alas, that real life dowry situations rarely do—with the guilty condemned.

Morever, if the medium is the message, it is sadly suspect, for the message is clearly this: how could such a sweet, young bride, the archetypal bahu, the willing doormat—how could even such a jewel of a girl be burnt to death? Throughout the film, this paradigm of the *ideal wife* remains monotonously unchanged, as if her martyr-like sacrifice of her own comfort for the comfort of her husband and his family somehow heightens the tragedy of her fate. Each act of inconceivable malice is countered with a fresh display of impossible goodness, sweetness and light. I find it significant, and disturbing, that the girl isn't less loving and milk-soppish, less of the archetypal, docile daughter-in-law, more spirited and unorthodox, or even just plain grumpy after several scenes of saintly endurance. It makes one feel that there is another, deeper, message within the film, viz. the unshakeable conviction that this is the way a 'good' daughter-in-law behaves.

This kind of stereotype, which is embedded deep in the creative consciousness, is one of the most dangerous among cultural prejudices because it is the most difficult to eradicate. The stereotype is all the more potent because it is superimposed with moral values which posit it as not merely virtuous and desirable, but also as representing everything that a long cultural tradition has sanctioned as necessary in a female. As a result, anything that even superficially digresses from this stereotype may be condemned as sinful, corruptive, and therefore undesirable. A trivial example is the way in which conservatism in dress continues to shape our ideas of what is decent or indecent. While Indian men have more or less uniformly adopted a broadly Western mode of dress, the women are still confined to wearing saris or, more recently, the North Indian salwar-kameez.

While this conservatism has more recently taken on a

new slant with the onslaught of the 'ethnic' cult, it still underscores a fundamental limitation of freedom in dress. It may be argued that the jeans-and-T-shirts generation is very much part of our scene now, but this would be true of only a very small section of even the urban population. Moreover, this 'freedom' is by and large tolerated *before* marriage. After marriage, for the most part, a woman is expected to revert to the more traditional forms of dress, especially on formal/religious occasions.

In many parts of India, even today, a girl in jeans or in forms of Western dress considered 'provocative' would send off a host of unintended signals to the opposite sex. She is automatically seen as being a certain 'type': brazen, loose and, worse, 'accessible'. The moral values implicit in such attitudes may be seen as part of the inbuilt resistance to *any* attempt to discard traditional patterns in a woman's lifestyle, of which the resistance to changes in dress is the most obvious.

Only recently, for instance, women students in a Calcutta college were warned that henceforth a dress code would be imposed on them. The principal claimed that such a code was 'part of a bigger movement to preserve the cultural values of the states, which were threatened with vulgarity and corruption by television'. The point here is, first, that the move would in no way rectify the alleged degeneration in media-values; second, what is more disturbing is the tacit assumption that *women* are especially susceptible to these degenerative forces. Needless to add, the principal's idea of 'appropriate dress' for women was the sari though he added, not surprisingly, that even the sari could be vulgar. He no doubt meant that the proper way to wear a sari was to bundle it loosely around oneself.

It is worth noting also, that while Bengali women's magazines have been reportedly urging their women readers to wear the salwar-kameez on the grounds that it is a more practical garment, the conventional attitude towards it has been guarded. Significantly, it is felt that the dress connotes an 'image . . . of aggressive modern women competing on terms of equality with men, because it allows greater freedom of movement and mobility'! ('Dress code for Calcutta college students', *Times of India*, 6 August 1993).

We now come to a more complex issue. If the Indian woman is by and large denied access to foreign modes of dress and if these in turn become symbolic of moral values or the lack of them, then what role do the more traditional, indigenous, modes of dress play? I shall take up some of the more common among those indigenous symbols whose relevance and validity is strictly female-defined. Among these, one of the most prevalent is the purdah. In a broad sense, purdah represents all the other symbols as well, because its implications are various and may not always be manifested through the actual wearing of purdah.

In other words, a physical symbol like purdah may signify a whole way of life and, in turn, incorporate several other modes of discrimination. 'Purdah', literally and etymologically, means 'curtain'. In the global context, it is commonly associated with the veil worn by women in many Islamic societies to hide their faces and bodies from the gaze of strangers. In other words, its gender-connotations are by and large known to people familiar with Muslim culture or with women-related issues. However, serious commentators have insisted on its etymological meaning as a more comprehensive indicator of its various functions, including the gender-related ones. Purdah, or curtain, literally signifies a concealment of what lies on the other side. Through such concealment, it grants privacy, secrecy, self-containment, and constructs a barrier between what it shields and the world outside.

The use of purdah is commonly seen as Islamic in origin, and in our own society there is perhaps some evidence for this view of the *widespread* practice of purdah as being post-Islamic. P. V. Kane cites several references in support of his contention that 'It is probably after the advent of the

Moslems that the wearing of a veil, which was not quite unknown, became general among Hindu women in Northern and Eastern India' (Vol.II, p. 598).

Kane quotes from the *Ṛg Veda*, X.85.33 and *Āśv. gr.* I.8.7, both of which imply that a bride wore no veil, since the spectators are asked to look upon her and bless her. The *Aitareya Brāhmaṇa* (12.11) suggests that some form of concealment was practised at home, in the presence of male in-laws, but Kane maintains that the wearing of a veil in public was not common and that it was restricted to women of royal birth.

This argument is borne out by the 'Ayodhyā-kāṇḍa' 33.8 and 116.28 of the *Rāmāyaṇa*. The former states that 'people walking on the public road see today Sītā who could not formerly be seen even by aerial beings', the latter that 'the appearance of a woman in public is not blamable in misfortunes, difficulties, in wars, in swayaṁvar, in a sacrifice, and in a marriage'. Another reference Kane gives is to the 'Sabhāparva'[15] 69.9 where Draupadī mentions the fact that she had never been seen in public by the kings since her swayaṁvar and laments her humiliation: 'we have heard that ancient people did not take married women to the public assembly hall; that ancient and long-standing practice has been contravened by the Kauravas' (Kane, p. 597). This *could* suggest that, purdah or no purdah, women did not participate freely in public gatherings.

'Sura' 24 ('Light'): 30 of the Koran is explicit about the need for concealment, but as Gail Papanek points out (*Separate World: Studies of Purdah in South Asia*, p. 23) the strictures here differ somewhat from the more commonly apprehended meaning of the word purdah—they mention the need to cover the bosom, but not the face. Believing women are asked to keep their eyes lowered and to conceal their *private parts* and their bosoms. They are asked not to reveal their attractions except for the external ones.

The metaphorical use of the term purdah as implying

the need to impose social seclusion and segregation on women is endemic to nearly all the cultures of the world and has manifested itself variously. Papanek comments on a strange difference in the practice of purdah among the Hindus and the Muslims: while the Muslim practice does not apply within the immediate family, purdah among the Hindus relates to the interaction of a woman with various male relatives (p. 5). This would fit in with the passage from the *Aitareya Brāhmaṇa* (12.11), referred to earlier. Papanek also draws our attention to the various codes of dress and behaviour, both Hindu and Muslim, which may be broadly classified as forms of purdah, since they emphasize 'the system of secluding women and enforcing high standards of female modesty in much of South Asia' (p. 5).

There is little doubt that such gender-discrimination operated rigorously in both the Hindu and Islamic cultures. This is borne out by the voices of radical, if sporadic, female protest. The sari-pallav is commonly associated with female modesty not merely by Hindus but also by the various other religio-cultural groups in India who have adopted the use of the sari. The pallav covers the breasts and, in conservative households, the head as well, particularly in the presence of males. The *positioning* of the sari-pallav, its proper use, thus came to indicate decency or the absence of decency in a woman.

These associational values were defied by the saint-poet Janābāī (Maharashtra, died 1350, date of birth not known):

The pallav over my head
has fallen onto my shoulders.
I shall go into the marketplace
crowded with people.
I shall carry
the cymbals in my hand,
the veena on my shoulders—
who can stop me now?

I shall set up trade
in the market of Pandharpur:
you may pour the oil
onto my wrist.
Jani says,
I have turned a prostitute, Lord,
I have set out for your home, Keshava.

In this poem Janābāī challenges the social codes which barred women and those of low birth from the right to public worship and salvation through the service of God. Janābāī was both. She belonged to the Śūdra caste, the lowest in the Hindu caste-hierarchy. The Śūdras, men and women, were automatically denied initiation privileges and, as a woman, Janābāī was even more removed from the possibility of access to the Vedas. She wryly comments on this double injustice in another poem where she tells God that he would have devotees only if he blessed them, because no one would serve him without reward. *The fact of being born as a woman/ should not depress me,* she adds, *it is the saints/ who have reduced Jani/ to this condition.*

Janābāī's forthright, no-nonsense tone indicates a clear understanding of how society would interpret her actions. Her strength lay in her ability to approach God and put Him to the test. If He, in fact, possessed all the qualities His devotees said He did, He should be able to see the irrational and unjust manifestations of social codes, and therefore to see through the game of social interpretation of individual behaviour.

Jani uses several images in her poem to signify her double oppression as a woman and as a Śūdra.[16] The pallav over her head which would suggest respectability has fallen onto her shoulders and remains there—a sure mark of brazenness. Undaunted, Jani will now go to the marketplace even though the prevalent norms of purdah (i.e. seclusion) made free movement in public questionable in a woman of virtue.

Worse, she takes the cymbals and the veena with her in a show of defiance, since these were musical instruments calculated to draw attention to herself—such exhibitionist abandon was not for women, but Jani in her shamelessness asserts that she will not be stopped. People are sure to brand her a fallen woman and she glories in her freedom through images of innuendo: she markets her trade and offers her wrist in a gesture reserved only for the prostitute she says she has now become. Jani has wholly abandoned herself to love of Kṛṣṇa and is indifferent to social mores and inhibitions. Her faith, and the fearless expression of it, matter more to her than her reputation.

The denial of learning to women could also be seen as a form of purdah. As already discussed, absence of education by keeping the oppressed ignorant and easy to exploit made the various practices of social segregation less easy to challenge. We have already referred to how the taboos attached to a biological process like menstruation in turn imposed a purdah within the purdah, segregation twice over, insisted upon in unambiguous if questionable terms.

If Janābāī had flouted womanly restrictions in her determination to serve God, Bahiṇābāī (Maharashtra, AD 1628–1700) encountered another form of male dominance because she, though a woman and a Brahmin, chose the low-caste Tukārām as her spiritual mentor. In her poetry, Bahiṇābāī describes her husband's inability to accept either her choice of the 'Śūdra Tukā' or her own exalted status as a woman of learning:

My husband says, we are Brahmins,
we sing the Vedas incessantly.
From where did the Śūdra Tukā
appear in her dreams?
My wife is ruined:
what shall I do now?
Who is this Jayarāma,[17] who this Pāṇḍuranga?[18]

The sanctity of my marriage
is now destroyed.

In her Introduction to *Separate Worlds* . . . , Hanna Papanek has summed up the functional role of purdah under two heads, 'two interacting and closely related principles which may be called, "separate worlds" and "provision of symbolic shelter" (p. 7). It is obvious however, that to a questioning mind like Bahiṇābāī's, such symbolic shelter was of little comfort. Bahiṇābāī's domestic world was overturned when she dared to draw aside the purdah which concealed the world of forbidden knowledge from women.

In the poem quoted above, Bahiṇābāī wonders what sins committed in an earlier birth had separated her from the supreme one in this one, and ironically accepts the superstitious belief that she has 'assumed human shape in a woman's form' only to bring 'countless sins to fruition'. She deplores the fact that she has no right to listen to expositions of the vedas, and that her own (Brahmin) caste forbids her knowledge of the Gāyatri mantra.[19] She lists the restrictions imposed on her as a woman, and says they have stifled her.

Ultimately however, Bahiṇābāī resolves to preserve her domestic world and attain God through what the Scriptures say:

To serve one's husband is to serve God:
the husband himself is the Almighty incarnate.
The husband is all holy places put together—
without that holiness, life has no meaning . . .
When he speaks, the Vedas speak . . .
Serving him will bring me true spiritual knowledge,
his interests are all my own.
If I worship any other god beside him
my soul will bear a guilt
as great as the sin of killing a Brahmin.
The husband is the guide, the means to salvation—

my resolution is true to heart.
Bahiṇi says, oh God,
your entry into my husband's mind
has made me firm and unwavering.

The irony in these lines can only be properly understood against the background of Hindu orthodoxy and belief: traditionally, marriage was the ritual which bore the same significance for women as the transformative ritual did for men. Manu (2.67) equated serving one's husband with serving a guru. When Manu's strictures are clear, each affirmation in the lines quoted is replete with a double meaning. Given the tenor of Bahiṇābāī's poetry as a whole, the lines obviously cannot be taken at face value. What is disturbing in our present day Indian context is that the sentiments are in fact more often than not taken at face value, are in fact still central to our ways of seeing. I doubt if most Indians would recognize the irony implicit in the lines: if they did, they would be anything but amused.

Bahiṇābāī's lament in her poetry, as a whole, was clearly against the unjust exclusion of women (even Brahmin women) from the life of the mind and from theological and religious knowledge. Such exclusion was by and large global, and successfully kept women in veils even if they did not wear any.

Recent studies of purdah have also shown that its observance does not indicate merely the practice of sexual discrimination but could also signify subtle social and class distinctions. In societies where it is worn, the cut, style and material would indicate the woman's status. In a class society, therefore, purdah not merely divides women from men but also amongst themselves. Moreover, while forms of purdah have existed throughout history, the insistence on actual physical purdah even today is a sad manifestation of the resurgence of feudal attitudes. It implies proprietary rights over one's woman/women, and is an affirmation of the need to impose stricter controls over them. This dismal view of female nature is unambiguously expressed. Abul A'la Maududi, the head of the Jamaat-i-Islami, sees the practice of purdah as a principal reason why 'the doors of a number of social and economic ills have been closed . . .' (Papanek, p. 26).

The *closed-minds* syndrome is particularly distressing because it tacitly accepts the most glaring injustices and sees them as given and unchangeable. Several examples of such a syndrome may be found in *Unveiling India: A Woman's Journey* by Anees Jung (Penguin India, 1990), a journalist and writer who had herself been brought up in purdah. Jung's book is a travelogue which describes a self-imposed journey through the physical and mental spaces of the Indian subcontinent, and records her encounters with the various faces of Indian orthodoxy. These include a visit to a Muslim household in Hyderabad where 'strict purdah' still operates. No woman from that house has ever stepped outside it, 'not even', the eldest brother tells Jung, 'to vote'. Jung observes that he says this with a note of self-satisfaction, as if he is 'recording a feat' (p. 32).

In an attempt to convince herself that the stranglehold of male diktat can be broken through female awareness and solidarity, Jung discusses the issue with an elderly woman in that house but meets with the same unfortunate resistance to change. Jung even reads aloud to her a verse from the Koran which decrees that 'The rule of modesty applies to both men and women . . . . The need for modesty is the same both in men and women' (p. 33). However, when Jung's attempt to convince the woman that the one-sided observance of purdah is arbitrary fails, it serves to confirm what she had earlier stated, viz. that purdah is primarily 'a state of mind' (p. 32).

It is this psychological sell (to borrow Greer's phrase) that poet Imtiaz Dharker also speaks of in describing purdah as 'a kind of safety'. Imtiaz Dharker is of Pakistani descent and spent her growing years in Britain. Much of the poetry in *Purdah* (Oxford University Press, 1989) is woman-centred and describes the experience of young immigrant girls faced with the tensions of the conflicting cultures of orthodoxy and a permissive society. Dharker visualizes purdah as hiding the body in the same way that the earth covers the coffins of dead men. In other words, purdah means the end of existence: it deadens the woman's capacity to interrelate with the world by inhibiting her sensory perception of it.

Moreover, besides rendering a woman's sensory existence dead, or at least confining/denying it, purdah also makes the woman a non-being, a person who is without an identity or individuality in the eyes of the external world. Papanek expresses this with a foreigner's reserve. Commenting on the tendency of outsiders to view women in burqas as 'non-persons', Papanek wonders whether the women themselves feel 'depersonalized' and whether those who interact with them see them as 'less than persons' (p. 14).

The fact remains that however well-presented a rationale which argues in favour of modes of dress/behaviour or for constraints on freedom of movement, thought or speech, their essential oppressiveness cannot be disguised: not when they are restricted to one-half the population of any country/culture and are defined in terms of gender alone. This is particularly so if they are maintained as unchangeable over a substantial period of human history when virtually everything else about the human condition is seen as subject to change, improvement and reform. The recent controversy over the issue of talaq or the Islamic code of divorce shows the paralysing effect of the practice of purdah.

The controversy was sparked off by a fatwa decreed by the Jamat-e-Ahle Hadis which is a non-political body. Issued in the last week of May 1993, it nullified the validity of the triple talaq as a means of divorce, when uttered at one go. While the over-all implications of the fatwa are not as far-reaching as they could have been (e.g., the pronouncement of talaq three times at monthly intervals is still held valid), what has been revealing is the attitude of several cross-sections of the community.

For example, it has been and is argued that, far from being exploitative, the practice signifies equality since it is open to both men and women to pronounce talaq. What is more to the point is how many women resort to it. The innumerable cases that come to light involve abandoned wives, not husbands, and the All India Muslim Women's Organization (AIMWO) has been agitating for reforms in the existing law ('Muslim women back fatwa on talaq', *Times of India*, 27 June 1993). According to Firoz Bakht Ahmed, grandson of Maulana Abul Kalam Azad and himself an educationist, 'The clergy is hardly bothered about the condition of Indian Muslim women, who constitute 50 per cent of the community's total population, 90 per cent of them being unlettered.' ('A separate identity', *The Indian Express, Sunday Magazine,* 11 July 1993). The AIMWO points out, for example, that even Islamic countries like Pakistan, Sudan, Turkey and Egypt have abolished the validity of a talaq pronounced three times at one sitting.

That the dreaded triple talaq can even be pronounced by registered post is apparent in the instance of Mumtaz Fazal Khan who is twenty-two and was divorced less than six months after her marriage because her parents were unable to pay up the two lakh rupees demanded as dowry. From the reported evidence, this case is even more indicative of the realities of our socio-cultural context. The husband who works in the Gulf, had apparently signed the papers even though he 'loves' his wife because his parents had asked him to do so, and he could not disobey them! The only positive aspect of this sordid story is the enlightened attitude of the girl's mother who is determined to use the incident to fight this evil ('A posted "talaq", a dream in tatters', *Times of India,* 31 July 1993).

Any form of oppression or exploitation can be

convincingly rationalized through selective quotation and calculated distortion. Thus, scoffing at the charge that the Bharatiya Janata Party is anti-woman, K. R. Malkani says: 'In the case of women they even combine two lies in one: they say that Hindu society has always ill-treated women and that BJP has very much inherited that tradition' ('Viewpoint', *Times of India,* 24 July 1993.)

What is worrying here is not merely whether or not the BJP has inherited the tradition, but the fact that Malkani can deny our inherently anti-woman world-outlook with such supreme confidence. Maintaining that Indian society has always accorded women a high place, he rails at the 'ignorant' who portray Manu as being anti-woman. In support of his argument that this charge is baseless, Malkani refers to Manu's statement that while a teacher may surpass ten sub-teachers in 'venerableness' and a father a hundred teachers, a mother surpasses a thousand fathers. He also quotes Manu's belief that the gods are present where women are honoured and that without such honour all rites are of no use. However, he ignores the fact that Manu says a great deal more. He denies a woman independence, says women are falsehood personified and unrestrainedly wanton, and makes their bondage mandatory on their menfolk—points which Malkani appears to conveniently overlook.

The question is whether any context is so fixed that its drawbacks cannot be subjected to rational review. This would apply in turn to the very reasons urged in support of certain social practices. If it is agreed that purdah in its various forms of manifestation is broadly representative of social restrictions on the free movement and behaviour of women, it should also be viewed in its essence as something which is man-imposed. Therefore, whatever the sociocultural, contextual reasons given to justify this restraint, any discussions about its validity would need to focus on remedial (and drastic) measures which seek to change the very conditions which make its practice seemingly so necessary.

That is, one needs to scrutinize whether purdah is regarded as essential because of a world-view that sees women as inherently corrupt or because the world they inhabit is so dangerous that they can only be safe if kept in bondage. If the latter, it can at best be a wishy-washy rationale as long as those conditions remain unaltered. There is every reason to insist therefore that the men who uphold the continuance of restrictive women-related laws/codes are only exploiting the women who are forced to observe them.

It is disturbing to find echoes of such dubious rationalizations in the emphasis among many present-day commentators, particularly the foreign ones, on the cocooning effects of purdah. This is particularly because they do not appear unaware of its sinister aspects. Rather, they appear to shy away from a critique which might lay them open to charges of 'outsider' hostility—a fear which seems vindicated if not justified when one reads local advocates of purdah like Rama Mehta. Mehta's attempt to soft-pedal the implications of purdah, even occasionally to romanticize it, may be seen in her article on 'Purdah Among the Oswals of Mewar' (Papanek, pp. 139–63). This supplements her earlier book on purdah. Mehta's article is of some interest because it deals with a form of Hindu purdah and is a theoretical study of a way of life which forms the substance of her Sahitya Akademi award-winning novel *Inside the Haveli*.

Mehta presents her case for the need for such an article, saying that the attempts of uninformed observers to run down the practices associated with purdah have created so much misunderstanding that it seems necessary to study purdah in a proper historical and sociocultural perspective (p. 140).

While there has been a great deal of misunderstanding about the purdah system, this is true about any practice which is culture-specific and subject to scrutiny by both insiders and outsiders. Such misunderstanding does not pre-empt seriousness of approach. Mehta's dismissive assumption that criticism of purdah implies its denigration by casual observers is difficult to accept *in toto*. Mehta, however, feels compelled to straighten the record and, in trying to present an allegedly unbiased analysis of the salutary effects of purdah, comes up with some rather startling assertions.

She begins with a brief account of the implications of purdah in the Hindu set-up. This reinforces Papanek's observation, quoted earlier, about the differing purposes of Hindu and Muslim purdah. Mehta explains that while purdah among the Muslims by and large relates to a woman's relationship with the world outside the home and begins at puberty, Hindu purdah generally has reference to a woman's role in her marital home and begins after marriage.

Speaking of the time when girls were married at puberty, Mehta justifies the double veil the daughter-in-law wore when moving outside the haveli on the grounds that it protected her from the pleasures and temptations of life. According to Mehta, the young girl's youthfulness made her susceptible to outside distractions, but her status as a new bride made it necessary for her to seek the approval of the mother-in-law for any activity. This approval was a safeguard against any 'emotional and psychological conflict' the girl may otherwise have experienced (p. 145).

There is no criticism here, implied or explicit, of a social system that first trapped a young girl not merely into marrying a total stranger but also into a relationship with a whole assembly of strangers and then thrust upon her a code of 'decorum' that crushed her freedom altogether. As already argued in my chapter on the girl-child, the reasons offered in support of girls marrying early are questionable on intellectual, social and sexist grounds. However, Mehta does not even admit these fallacies. Instead she sets out to persuade us that the blinkered existence she advocates kept women psychologically and emotionally stable! There is very little difference between such a stand and the arguments of the conservative law-givers who would defend virtually any practice on the grounds that the situation demanded it.

In fact Manu, who had maintained that a woman was not fit for independence and that her promiscuous nature demanded that man guard her to the utmost, would appear to have an ardent supporter in Rama Mehta who defends the traditionalist practice of constraining a young bride in order to guard her from temptation and to keep her mother-in-law happy! Mehta even insists on the purdah and the haveli as moulding a young bride's dignity and giving her the self-confidence with which *she* would one day run the haveli. It would be rather more realistic to see this as a self-perpetuating exercise in seeing the lifestyle of women in cloistered and restricting terms. After all, in commenting on the decline of purdah towards the end of her essay, even Mehta admits that 'the very rigidity of purdah proved to be its greatest frailty' (p. 153).

These contradictions in her argument do not however appear to have fazed Mehta who has also glorified the practice of purdah in the award-winning novel *Inside the Haveli*. Her protagonist in this novel seems almost a tailor-made sample of the daughter-in-law stereotype which Mehta's essay had defended. Entering the haveli as a young, rebellious bride, Geeta matures through the novel to the position of proud mistress of the haveli. However, Geeta is prone to sentimental lapses even in her earlier rebellious phase. She is actually shown as being filled with 'a glow of pride and affection' when she contemplates the glory of the family. She forgets her daily irritations and feels a sense of pride in her role as the young mistress of the haveli. She rebukes herself for having allowed little pinpricks to blind her to the greatness of their family traditions.

This incident takes place during a family get-together when Geeta sneaks away from the women's quarters and secretly observes the men who are clustered together in their part of the house. This hallowing of stultifying practices by means of uncritical references to past glories, traditions and saṁskāras is, unfortunately, a national weakness with us. Nirad C. Chaudhuri, in pointing out this tendency, is rightly sceptical about the value of such a past, or its reality and validity in present-day terms. His view is that, to a large number of Indians, their historic civilization is merely something with which they hope to score a point over foreigners—their 'cultural consciousness' is 'part of their nationalism' ('Adventures of a Brown Man in Search of Civilization', in *A Passage to England*, Macmillan, London, 1959, p. 157).

Geeta's emotionalism, which mirrors that of her creator, ignores the fundamental principle behind the existence of an institution like the haveli. The question is not whether the haveli looks after the women and shelters them, but whether it cannot be made superfluous by changing the way things work so that women no longer remain weak/helpless/in need of protection.

In the same article, Mehta also writes of the haveli's role in helping to maintain the dignity of the child-widow. She mentions the term with astonishing ease, its dark horrors appear to escape her. *Child-widow*? Was it necessary for such a person to exist at all? Yet child-widows did exist, and were doomed in our culture to an existence even more dreadful than that which someone widowed in the natural course of time endured and still does.

My own grandmother was barely more than a child when she was widowed, at the age of nineteen. She had two children: my mother who was four when this happened, and my uncle who was three. I have heard enough about the life of both my grandmother and my mother to be sceptical about the alleged benefits of a system that permitted a young girl to be widowed merely because it saw an early marriage as a means to the fulfilment of her existence.

My grandmother's life was both typical and a-typical. Though married very young, she had a husband who helped her educate herself and encouraged her to learn to become intellectually independent. Unfortunately, he did not live long. A doctor with the Indian Medical Services, he was on deputation to the armed forces in the First World War and died at sea when his ship was torpedoed by the Germans. His family had been expecting him home in the New Year: what they got instead was the news of his death.

My grandmother could have given up all that he had helped her to believe in and surrendered to family pressures. She chose to keep her independence and continued to live on her own with her young children. She managed on a widow's pension and even looked after her sister's children. She sent both her children abroad and continued with her own study. She read avidly, and it was she who introduced me to Tolstoy and Jane Austen. When she died at seventy-eight, she could speak, read, and write four languages (Marathi, English, Kannada and Telugu) and was learning a fifth (Bengali).

I refer to my grandmother because of Mehta's summary mention and dismissal of something that was more than a social statistic to me: a child-widow. My grandmother may have been a woman who opted out of the silken web of family-shelter but she paid the price in social terms for being what is unforgivable in our social set-up: a widow. Her price was the more exacting because she was a young widow with a young daughter. It would be impossible to detail the numerous anecdotes my mother had to tell, the innumerable subtle blows that left their mark even when she was an adult. I refer to some of these in my next chapter where they seem to arise out of the context. I need only add that my own perception of various forms of social discrimination in relation to my grandmother made me sceptical, even as a child, of all the baubles and the romanticized fiddle-faddle concerning Indian womanhood, female apparel and adornment.

Chapter 4

Vaidhavya

(Widowhood)

From earliest times, such joy in existence as was permitted a woman was supposed to end with the death of her husband. Nearly all the texts are agreed in prescribing rigorous forms of abstinence for a widow, though the duration of such periods of abstinence varied according to different interpretations (Kane, p. 538).

Manu is clear on this point. He states that a widow should remain celibate and forbearing till her death. She is graciously permitted to fast as much as she likes, is prescribed a vegetarian diet, and is warned against even mentioning another man's name. Chastity, restraint and life-long endurance are the other qualities she is advised to cultivate, but on no account can a 'virtuous woman' ever marry again (5.157-8, 162). In contrast, a 'twice-born man who knows the law' is not merely permitted to take a second wife after he has performed the last rites of the first: he is *actually exhorted to do so*. Manu cautions him against neglecting his duties as a householder, and these duties require him to marry again (5.169, p. 116).

The responsibilities of gṛhasthāśrama were well-suited to the male world-order. This is obvious from the fact that a second marriage was seen as necessary for a man if he were to be able to fulfil his obligations as a householder. Since the woman had no such obligations except as her husband's partner, all her rights to such rituals ceased anyway once she was widowed. It was the son who was then appointed to carry on these duties, a practice which still prevails. Given the emphasis our society places, for better or for worse, on such rituals, the highly discriminatory flavour of this gender-bound access to them even today needs drastic rectification: unless we move for change, time present and time past will continue unchanged in time future.

I was thirty-eight when my father died, and at the twelfth day śrāddha, performed to supposedly ensure his soul a peaceful transition into the other world, the reality of what was happening seemed so obvious that I was surprised no one else who had been close to him could see it. As the ceremony progressed, my mother's deliberate and ritualistic exclusion from its various stages made the whole exercise a mockery, a triumph of blind ritual over the purpose and relevance of what it symbolized.

Something snapped within me finally, when I heard the priest explicitly forbid my brother to offer my mother something that was being carried around to everyone else. All the stories I had heard about my grandmother, everything my father himself had told me about the treatment of widows in orthodox Hindu society, seemed crystallized into that one moment. I only remember that I left the room at this point and refused to return even though the priest sent my brother to warn me that this rebellious gesture in my mother's support would hinder the safe passage of my father's soul!

My father had been as ideal a husband as is humanly possible. Men of his generation, his so-called friends, colleagues and even his students jeered at him behind his back, called him 'hen-pecked' (another loaded term used to refer to men who allow their wives independence of thought and spirit). He saw his marriage as a true partnership, never took my mother for granted, helped her around the house, looked after the house every evening so that she could attend her clinic. Not hurting my mother had become an obsessive need with my father. He had even told me once, during his last fatal illness, that he had wanted her to die before him only because he didn't want her ever to know the pain and unjust horror of Indian widowhood: the kind he had heard my grandmother talk about and which my mother had witnessed as a child because of *her* mother's condition as a widow. Yet, at this ceremony, allegedly performed to guarantee his soul eternal peace, we were being exhorted to do the very things which would surely give it eternal torment. It amazed me that no one could see such blatant irony.

It was my father's wish that, if widowed, my mother would always continue to wear the kumkum and, with some coaxing, I persuaded her to do so. But she never wore the mangal-sūtra again. Though there was none of the hysterical breaking of bangles etc., I can still remember the moving dignity of the moment when she silently went into the bathroom and had a bath after which she emerged without all the accoutrements which had been a constant part of her apparel, unusual woman though she was, since the day she was married.

The pressures motivating such an action have their roots in the Śāstras which have outlined innumerable strictures regulating the conduct of widows. All these drive home the fact that a widow's lot was an unenviable one. 'She should give up adorning her hair, chewing betel-nut, wearing perfumes, flowers, ornaments and dyed clothes, taking food from a vessel of bronze, taking two meals a day, applying collyrium to her eyes . . . ' (*Vṛddha Hārita*, XI 205–10).

A widow had to wear white, to curb her impulses and emotions, to sleep on a mat of kuśa grass. A widow who slept on a cot was actually charged with sending her husband's soul to hell! ('Kāśīkhaṇḍa' of the *Skandapurāṇa*,[1] chapter 4). According to the *Skandapurāṇa* (III, Brahmāraṇya section, chapter 7, verses 50–51), the widow was 'more inauspicious than all other inauspicious things'. The sight of the widow meant certain failure in any undertaking. Except for one's own widowed mother, all other widows were tainted with this characteristic of inauspiciousness. The wise man was warned to 'avoid even their blessings like the poison of a snake' (all references from Kane, pp. 584–85.)

The way the 'typical' caught up with my grandmother many years ago was contained in the many horrendous stories my mother told me. One of these was the scene she witnessed between *her* mother and grandmother (i.e. my great-grandmother) a few days after the news of my grandfather's death was received. My grandmother was apparently resisting the pressure to have her head tonsured in accordance with convention. She succeeded eventually, but my mother said she would never forget the way my grandmother had had to scream. Her words ('Not before the child! Don't bring this up before the child!') haunted my mother all her life.

My grandmother's experience in this respect needs to be looked at in its historical/cultural context for several reasons. It was believed that a widow who braided her hair thereby kept her husband in bondage ('Kāśīkhaṇḍa' of the *Skandapurāṇa*). Therefore it was necessary for her to shave her head! According to P.V. Kane, there is evidence to suggest that the passages in the *Skandapurāṇa* relating to the duties of widows were later interpolations (p. 586). In support of his argument, Kane points out (p. 588) that Manu and Yājñavalkya-smṛti[2] are silent on this matter. Moreover, the fact that texts like *Vṛddha Hārita* ask the widow not to adorn her hair indicates that women were not expected to tonsure themselves. Kane suggests that the idea may have come from the example of Buddhist and Jain nuns. Buddhist nuns cut their hair and wore orange robes; till fairly recently Brahmin widows in Maharashtra tonsured their heads and wore a reddish garment (pp. 592–93).

However, what *is* certain is that at some stage the

tonsuring of widows was seen as prescribed and the practice became rampant. To me this only makes the practice even more despicable, for it suggests that the smṛtis were observed only when it suited men to do so. This is especially so with regard to the status and treatment of women: when necessary, the minds of men have created and perpetuated a whole new system of codes and practices calculated to humiliate women and keep them socially impotent.

Whatever the reasons therefore for the origin of practices like the tonsuring of widows, they only accentuate the unequal basis of the male-female relationship. Other such strictures involve the restrictions on forms of food like meat. My mother, who was a vegetarian, once told me that she had been very fond of non-vegetarian food as a child: 'When it wasn't cooked at home any more, I'm told your uncle and I used to cry for it. Later, I forgot that I had ever eaten it. Now, I've no desire to.' She didn't have to say any more for me to wonder what socio-religious compulsions can reduce a four-year-old and a three-year-old to craving for a particular item of food merely because their father is dead. The hold of these strictures over the popular consciousness is evident in the way widows are regarded in Indian society even today. My mother-in-law recently told me how she was solicitously led to a separate part of a wedding where a different, bland, widow-appropriate (vegetarian) menu was being proffered.

Similar prejudices about widows meant that they could never participate in that most basic Maharashtrian ritual, the haldi-kumkum. While I would objectively regard haldi-kumkum as hardly the most exciting of social events, they are in this sense a vicious and sinister perpetuation of a cruel code observed by women even though it clearly denies another woman the right to live with dignity. This deliberate exclusion of widows from even such all-female rituals is still very much in practice.

The kumkum itself is one of several symbols of gender-discrimination: sindoor, the colours red and green, bangles, nose and toe rings, anklets, mehndi, āltā and so on. All these constitute a rigid code of bondage which is solely female-circumscribed. Yet, without exception, they are imbued with suggestions of romance, lyricism, beauty, enchantment, fulfilment etc. Their darker implications are conveniently ignored even by persons with allegedly radical views.

The associational values of romance and beauty contained in these symbols are enhanced in various ways by the media. The advent of consumerism has of course further reduced woman's commodity-status to one coloured by the dubious connections between the product being marketed and a woman's desirability. That this is unfortunately a global disease is borne out by the innumerable references made to the pervasive power of such forms of 'psychological sell' (Greer, *The Female Eunuch*, p. 81). And elsewhere, Sara M. Evans (*Born for Liberty,* The Free Press, New York, Collier Macmillan Publishers, London, 1989) comments on the aggressive if insidious manner in which American advertising during the Cold War era linked sexual attractiveness to marital prospects (p. 248).

Evans points out that the feminine mystique which was consolidated during these years had already 'wedded prewar ideas about the centrality of home-making and motherhood' to more popularized versions of Freudian sexuality, producing 'a sexualized, modernised version of republican motherhood' (p. 246). To this was added the message of sexuality-oriented consumerism, evident in advertising slogans such as the following: 'She's engaged! She's lovely! She uses Pond's!'; or 'Camay, for skin that says, "I do!"' (p. 248).

In this sense, therefore, it is not surprising that our own brand of media-moulded consumerism aims at those emotional nerve-centres which can be relied upon to trigger a collective response. A highly glamorized Indian television commercial for a skin-cream relies on the tradition of smearing a bride-to-be with turmeric. She is then shown seated coyly, wearing her bridal finery of red and gold. In innumerable Indian films, that moment when a bridegroom applies the kumkum or the sindoor in the parting of his bride's hair is one which is charged with high drama and romance: shenais commonly split the air with rāgas which ooze moods of sentimental longing, and tears of joy are shed all round.

However, there is also the counterpart to this joyous moment: when a woman is widowed. She could be either a young widow or an old one. Like the wedding-scene described earlier, this one is in turn fraught with high drama—the melodramatic breaking of the chudiyaan, the glass bangles which symbolize marital bliss. As already pointed out in my first chapter, even Shyam Benegal's progressive ideology was not immune to the stereotyped aura of such moments, which are exploited to the fullest in a film like *Junoon*.

The auspicious associations attached to the colour red are clearly related to the process of bridal defloration (signifying chastity) and its implications of fertility and child-bearing. The colour red symbolizes the rupture of the hymen and the husband's access thereby to his wife's body which is in turn seen as a field awaiting fructification. The same idea informs the wearing of green bangles and a green sari at the time of marriage. As Sindhu S. Dange points out, pre-wedding rites have been given a significant name in the Vedic tradition: indrāṇī-karma. Dange clarifies the term by explaining that Indrāṇī stands for tillable land in the *Ṛg-Veda*—the bride therefore is one such tillable land which will be fructified by the bridegroom ('Symbolism of the Ceremonial Rituals', in *Indian Symbology*, Proceedings of the Seminar on Indian Symbology held at the Industrial Design Centre on 17, 18, 19 January 1985, ed. Kirti Trivedi, Industrial Design Centre, January 1987, p. 85).

Red and green, colours associated with fertility and marriage, demarcated female roles within marriage and were reserved, in the context, exclusively for the the wife. While, in course of time, they have come to be used by young, unmarried girls (the kumkum tikka on the forehead is now generally of the artificial, stick-on variety and comes in several designs and shades) they significantly remain taboo for widows. The widow who wears the traditional kumkum mark on her forehead does so in defiance of social norms—the fact that more and more widows are now doing so has not had any effect on the conservative majority view which would regard such a liberty as a blatant transgression against the code of the Śāstras.

Similar taboos for widows include rites such as the applying of patterned mehendi designs on the hands and feet and of the red āltā on the feet. A woman I know was made to dip her feet in a bowl of red alta on her wedding-day. She was then made to stand on a large white cloth so that the imprint of her feet were recorded and put away. This practice, resembling the fingerprinting of criminals, is reportedly a relic of the old times: prints of the young bride's feet were recorded in this way so that she could be traced if she had the guts to run away. The incident I witnessed took place in the late nineteen seventies.

In my first chapter, I had referred to Bṛhaspati's[3] devastating definition of the true pativratā. The definitions of the pativratā are found in several texts, and while they differ marginally in their details they all emphasize her existence as being husband-bound.

The *Skandapurāṇa* ('Brahma-khaṇḍa', 'Dharmāraṇya section', chapter 7) states that a pativratā should always use haldi (turmeric), kumkum, sindoor, outline her eyes with lamp black, braid her hair, and wear a bodice, tāmbūla and auspicious ornaments (vv. 28-29). According to the Padma-purāṇa (Srsti-khaṇda, chapter 47, v. 55), a pativratā was like a slave when at work, a courtesan when making love, like a mother when serving food, and a counsellor when the husband was in distress (Kane, p. 565). It was also emphasized that, in the husband's absence from home, the woman was expected to give up the prescribed adornment of her body.

The maṅgal-sūtra, tied by the husband round the bride's neck during the marriage-ceremony, is another gender-based symbol of matrimony. P.V. Kane points out (p. 537) that the sūtras are silent about this ritual, while even the smrtis are devoid of any mention of the nose-ring. Any attempt to analyse all these practices should take into account the fact that they not merely imply gender-discrimination but, worse, that they are accessible to a married woman *only as long as her husband is alive*. A woman, once widowed, is willy-nilly compelled to stop wearing them. As against this, there are no binding symbols of matrimony in relation to a husband/widower. Thus these become discriminatory twice over.

Of the various fates that could/can befall a woman, widowhood was/is considered to be the most unfortunate. The most blessed fortune a woman could/can hope for was/is to precede her husband into the grave, to die a suhaagan, with the red in the parting of her hair or on her forehead intact. It is this inextricable bonding of a woman's 'fate' to her husband's being alive or dead that Bahiṇābāī Choudhari[4] (Maharashtra, 1880–1951) ironically refers to in one of her poems, when she mocks the palmist for trying to locate her fate-line on her palm:

> The fate-line is hidden
> beneath the kumkum on my forehead:
> the kumkum wiped away,
> the fate-line is revealed . . .

It will be granted by virtually all Indians that this state of perception is not one which is as yet past or done with. The suhaagan mystique still dominates our responses and ways of feeling. Television renditions of our two most influential texts, the *Rāmāyaṇa* and the *Mahābhārata*, creations of the late nineteen eighties, embodied this concept of ideal wifehood through the blessing 'Sowbhāgyavati bhava', conferred on all the women by their elders.

It could, of course, be argued that through the persistence in having this particular blessing articulated so frequently and enthusiastically, the makers of these serials were merely ensuring that their characters were faithful to the temporal context of these two epics. However, this argument would not explain the fact that this blessing is heard frequently enough in *today's* context as well. Moreover, it is significant that while these televised versions professed their intention to circumvent anachronisms in the standard text in various ways (Sītā's second banishment being the result of *her* choice rather than Rāma's blinkered sense of honour and justice, for instance), the only concepts which not merely remained untouched but were even glorified were those relating to the status and role of women, especially wives.

The superstitious fear attached to any defiance of strictures as regards widows may be witnessed even today. In spite of the fate of *some* widows being considerably better, it is obvious that these are individual instances and are in no way indicative of fundamental changes in attitudes. Moreover, while some widows may have more freedom or more spirit than others, the social taboos catch up with them even today, the way they did with my grandmother so many years earlier. Widows are by and large regarded as *unholy*. At best, they are people to be tolerated but not allowed more than a token endurance of their presence.

The ghāts at Varanasi and the temples at Puri are graphic reminders of the pitiable plight of a large number of widows driven out by orthodox society. These women are forced to spend their lives as abhorred destitutes. Every now and again there are battles fought in courts of law about the rights of a widow in her own home. Occasionally, horrendous tales of actual physical abuse are reported.

The arbitrary manner in which a widow is denuded of

all the external symbols of matrimony (dubious as these are) is not only grossly unfair and cruel but also clearly contradictory. On the one hand, she is psychologically coerced into regarding herself as still married to her dead husband. She is warned that she is responsible for the peace of her husband's soul. On the other hand, the very signs of marriage, which had been gifted to her at the time of marriage, and which for the believing woman would unconditionally signify the sanctity of this relationship of eternal bondage, are taken away from her. Red and green are now taboo colours. She is even forbidden the use of other bright colours and must wear white or muted shades. For, 'just as birds flock to a piece of flesh left on the ground, so all men woo [or try to seduce] a woman whose husband is dead' ('Ādiparva' 160.12, Kane p. 584.)

In other words here, as always, the *woman* is forcibly given the onus of preventing what is essentially, if allegedly, the manifestation of *male* licentiousness. As with the various forms of purdah, traditionalists as far-ranging as the ancient law-makers and the present-day Malkanis and Rama Mehtas would argue that these restraints on the widow are aimed at her protection. The same rationale would be used to explain why widows were pronounced to be irredeemably inauspicious. Several apologists of orthodoxy would no doubt maintain that such pronouncements were made to prevent men from sexually exploiting a widow. The fact remains, however, that it would have been more appropriate, even fairer, to regard as inauspicious, or harmful, or disruptive of social harmony the *men* who may have actually exploited a vulnerable woman in this way. There seems no justification for the need to tarnish a widow's morals in this way merely to camouflage the questionable feudal manner in which women have been generally viewed, with seeming impunity.

In spite of the innumerable references in Indian literature to these inhuman attitudes towards widows, most taboos surrounding them continue. In Anita Desai's novel *Clear*

Light of Day (Allied Publishers, Bombay, 1980), the widowed Mira-māsi is a stereotypical example of the Indian widow. Desai refers to the fact that it was her desiccated physique which had spared her from being sexually abused by her brothers-in-law, but that this did not prevent them from eyeing her disparagingly and making insulting remarks (p. 108).

There are other forms of economic and social exploitation to which a widow was subjected, and which the Śāstras have actually sanctioned. The inheritance rights of widows were practically non-existent in ancient times. Even today, it is tacitly assumed that a widow would surrender her rights in favour of her *sons,* not her *daughters*.

While, as already noted, *social obligations* made it incumbent on a widower to marry again, the very same world-view compelled a widow to remain celibate. *Vedavyāsa-smṛti* II.53 states that a 'brāhmaṇa woman should enter fire, clasping the dead body of her husband; if she lives (does not become sati) she being *tyaktakeśā* should emaciate her body by *tapas*' (Kane, p. 589). Kane gives several textual evidences to support his argument that *tyaktakeśā* ('who has given up hair') cannot imply the tonsuring of widows. However, what is of interest now, since the question of tonsuring has been discussed earlier in this chapter, is the reference to sati.

Kane points out that the practice of widow burning is to be found among the ancient Greeks, Germans, Slavs and other races (p. 625). He is also categorical about the fact that there is no Vedic passage which would incontrovertibly prove that the practice was current in India. According to him, there is no hard and fast evidence then as to whether the practice arose indigenously or was borrowed. None of the Dharmasūtras except *Viṣṇu* contain any reference to it. Even this reference is not prescriptive of the practice in any absolute sense: 'On her husband's death the widow should observe celibacy or should ascend the funeral pyre after him'

(Kane, p. 626). Kane's deduction, from the available sources, is that the practice was originally restricted to royal families and that it was rare even amongst them. Further, according to him, it would appear that the practice began among the Kṣatriyas and spread to the Brahmins much later.

Whatever the historical reasons for the origin of this practice, it is evident that it came to acquire a certain social charisma. The example of the Rajput queens who immolated themselves to escape sexual abuse at the hands of the invading conquerors may have its own validity. What is questionable is the transformation of such incidents into a myth exalting female valour and chastity. The implication then is not merely that these women had a rare degree of fortitude and prized their chastity above life itself, but that those women who do not subscribe to this alternative either lack fortitude or, worse, would rather live to be raped and abused: a choice which is colourfully contained in the global euphemism 'a fate worse than death'. Surely a system wherein the behaviour of men necessitates that a widow immolate herself to preserve her sexual dignity deserves censure for its indulgence of male feudalism rather than praise for the so-called purity of its women. Failure to admit this implies that the right to live unmolested and with dignity is something no woman/widow within such a system could expect.

Moreover, it was only a matter of time before the change from perceiving the act as a social necessity (if a morally questionable one) to seeing it as essential, even binding, took place. A sati came to be seen as possessing an immeasurable degree of moral merit. She could absolve her husband of the most heinous of sins, including the killing of a Brahmin! She was also equipped with the moral power to purify three families: those of her mother, her father and her husband (Kane, p. 631).

At the same time, it should be noted that early commentators were generally against the practice. Several scholars, including Kane, argue that the practice of sati was sporadic and that relatives and family members tried to dissuade a widow from resorting to it. However, the general censure of widows along with their humiliation and degradation, as well as the rapaciousness of the surviving relatives on the husband's side may, in several cases, have resulted in a degree of implicit or explicit coercion.

Nayantara Sahgal's novel *Rich Like Us* (William Heinemann, 1985, Sceptre edition, 1987; my references are from the third impression of this edition, 1993) was published long before the much-publicized resurgence of sati with the Roop Kanwar episode. In this novel, the protagonist Sonali discovers a manuscript written by her paternal grandfather in 1915. It is, to begin with, an account of various conversations overheard, between *his* father and a Mr Timmons, the British Resident in the state. A large part of this conversation deals with sati, but there is also a frightening description of an actual incident of sati—that of his own mother.

Widowed, she asks her young son to fetch Mr Timmons, her dead husband's friend, to ensure that her son's inheritance in safe. But Mr Timmons is away, and before he can return the widow is already a memory, burnt alive by the same relatives who had used a brick to break the glass bangles on her wrists. This is well after the funeral. The widow's son, who has been attending classes in college, returns to an empty house. Some premonition drives him to the river bank where he sees a new pyre blazing. He sees his mother 'fling her arms wildly in the air, then wrap them about her breasts before she subsided like a wax doll into the flames' (p. 149).

The obsessive preoccupation with sati in the manuscript makes it an extremely well-researched document. It contains several newspaper accounts from the early nineteenth century, of the ways in which widows were forcibly kept in the flames even when they struggled to escape. The writer's own father describes to Mr Timmons how women were intoxicated and sedated before they were dragged off to become satis, so that they were insensible to their physical pain and did not scream when the flames engulfed them. The narrator's father had once rushed to a village on hearing of an incident of sati and had come home to describe how 'The people had been in an ecstasy of revival' (p. 142).

Rich Like Us was published two years *before* the Roop Kanwar incident, but it was an eerie portent of the mass hysteria her act aroused. As in the novel, the people were clearly in an 'ecstasy of revival'. While some of the intelligentsia expressed horror, a sufficiently large number of people expressed admiration. Several hundreds of people are reported to have thronged to her village in Rajasthan to witness the event. In spite of the official insistence that the thirteenth day ceremony would not be allowed to take place, it did. In *Whose News? The Media and Women's Issues* (Sage Publications, New Delhi, 1994), editors Ammu Joseph and Kalpana Sharma refer to journalist Vishal Mangalwadi's coverage of Roop Kanwar's chunri mahotsav in *The Indian Express* of 19 September 1987. Mangalwadi quoted people who were present at her death, 'vividly documenting the horror of a young girl being buried alive under firewood, screaming for help, receiving none and the fire being re-lit to ensure her end, with crowds of people watching all the while' ('The Roop Kanwar Tragedy: In The Name of Tradition', p. 74).

Worse, the official ban has meant the absence of authentic newspaper accounts. Roop Kanwar, reportedly, has already become a legend. Glorified and sanctified in popular memory, photomontages of her smilingly immolating herself, clad in all her bridal finery, flood the local market. It is even rumoured that a shrine has sprung up in her memory.

Sati was legally prohibited in 1829 by the British Governor Lord Bentinck. Though its occurrence was less frequently noticed after the official outlawing, occasional satis were not unknown. Nayantara Sahgal admits that her great-grandmother became a sati. (*The Tribune, Saturday*

Plus, Chandigarh, 24 December 1988). My own family boasted of a sati, and there is even a shrine to mark the spot in the courtyard of my great-uncle's ancestral home in Bandivde, Sindhudurg. Roop Kanwar's act highlighted the revivalist potential of this phenomenon. The enormous mass support she received in Rajasthan gave sati a new, dangerous dimension. It hinted at the distorting power of fundamentalist tendencies masked as community-pride.

The Commission of Sati (Prevention) Act, 1987, passed by Parliament in 1988, was an attempt to provide a more stringent deterrent to the practice of sati. However, the Act has several questionable loop-holes, the principal one being its ambiguity as regards the culpability of the respective parties involved. The qualitative difference between the woman as victim, even if a *willing* one, and those who assist her in the act is either not perceived or not clearly demarcated. No allowances are made for the fact that a woman's apparent willingness may in fact be the product of other forces: brainwashing, psychological blackmail, superstitious fear or glorification and so on. Similarly, in treating the sati and the instigators as equally culpable, the Act betrays a surprising insensitivity to, and blindness as regards, the very sociocultural reality which it ostensibly seeks to transform.

Even if sati is legally prohibited, there are several other indignities similar to it which have private if not legal sanction. While sati involves the burning of a widow when her husband dies, present-day experience points to the increasing evidence that there are other more horrific forms of handling unwanted wives. Many of them are burnt while he is still alive. Nandita Gandhi and Nandita Shah enumerate some of the more publicized instances of bride-burning, harassment and murder (pp. 54–8). It may be safely assumed that an average dose of mental and physical abuse is discreetly accepted by most women and hardly ever gets talked about. While violence against middle-class women may be occasionally reported in the press, there are large numbers of economically deprived women who accept violence at the hands of their men as natural and unalterable. Women who work as domestic helps in many urban homes nearly all have harrowing stories to narrate, of wife-bashing, child-abuse, infidelity and rape. These are the living satis. They are part of the syndrome which has produced and condones the other kind.

Chapter 5

Dowry

Violence may be triggered off by greed. Many of the harassment cases concerning young married women are dowry-related. In spite of the laws prohibiting dowry, the expectation that it would be given persists. It is assumed by many Indians that the bride's parental home is like the proverbial magic pitcher: it has an infinite capacity to produce more, no matter how often it is emptied. The institution of dowry, i.e. the handing over, on demand, of gifts in cash and kind by the bride's family to the bridegroom's as a pre-condition to marriage, is itself of dubious origin, but has come to be accepted as a sacrosanct privilege even by supposedly enlightened men.

Manu unambiguously warned that no one, not even a servant, ought to accept a bride-price for his daughter, for a man who did so was covertly selling his daughter. Manu emphatically stated that bride-price did not exist even in earlier times, and also disapproved of the practice of promising a girl to one man and then giving her to another (Manu, 9.98-100).

It should be noted that Manu refers to the *bride-price*, i.e. to a price received by the father of the *bride*. Even this practice, moreover, is condemned on the grounds that it implied a 'covert' sale of the daughter. At some stage in our history, however, this practice was reversed so that it became common to offer a price for the bridegroom rather than for the bride. This has in turn developed into the notorious dowry or marriage-portion gifted to the bridegroom and his family when a girl is given in marriage.

Though the giving of dowry is legally forbidden, it is common knowledge that a price is expected, frequently named, and ruthlessly exacted from the father of the bride. The form in which dowry is given may vary, but certain uniform features are apparent. In today's consumeristic world these include ornate saris and/or jewellery for the women in the bridegroom's family; acquisitions such as TV sets, refrigerators, mixers, furniture, a car/scooter; cash gifts, and a non-stop flow of commodities at every festival, particularly when the set-up is that of a joint family.

In spite of the persistent campaign against dowry, such undercover giving and receiving seems unaffected. The bride's father gives according to his means, frequently out of proportion to them, borrowing if necessary, since he believes that his daughter's prestige and happiness are at stake. Ironically, no one who is party to such a transaction appears to wonder what happiness measured in these terms implies, or whether it exists at all, or is worth acquiring at that price. The spectre of having one's daughter rejected and unmarried or worse, of having the marriage called off at the eleventh hour if the price paid does not match the expectation seems to deaden the scepticism of the most self-avowedly progressive fathers. Once married, girls are coerced into asking their fathers for additional gifts and tortured if these are not forthcoming. In some cases, they are ruthlessly done away with.

The sad truth in most such cases is that the girls murdered for dowry have reportedly tried to apprise their parents of the way things are only to be told to endure their torturers in silence. The repercussions of having a married daughter return to her father's home are usually too overwhelming for these parents, making them unwilling to face the risk. These repercussions include the gossip of neighbours and the community, the sense of humiliation and shame, the possibility that such an eventuality would jeopardize the marriage-prospects of their other daughters by affecting the family honour, and so on.

The eventual ill-treatment and murder of the girl grieves them. There are scenes of self-reproach, but unfortunately these do not add up to any significant change in attitude. Dowry-related deaths have received considerable attention, but they have not been eye-openers in any revolutionary sense, since dowry is still demanded, discreetly or blatantly, and given. The going rate depends on the boy's profession, and his consequent value in the marriage market.

With characteristic crassness, dowry has even become something of an in-joke among urban men of marriageable age. Such humour is seen as a sign of sophistication. The girl/woman who marries one of these men is expected to take these 'social realities' for granted, as if they are so natural and unchangeable that her responses ought not to indicate that she sees them as revolting or questionable. A woman I know recently told me how, a couple of days after they were married, she and her husband met a former college-friend of his who jabbed her husband in the ribs, pointed to his new trousers and asked him audibly, in her presence, whether they were part of what he termed 'the loot'. This remark was hugely appreciated by the others present.

Several people I know would argue that this was only a 'joke', and that this woman was being unnecessarily touchy in finding it offensive ('women's libbers' aren't supposed to have a sense of humour, remember? They're always far too earnest). The fact is that as a joke the statement was in outrageously bad taste, first, because dowry itself is not funny; and second, to the individual who made the joke, at any rate, dowry was apparently serious business, one of the perks of being an Indian male, a practice that could and should be used to exploit the wife's family. Worse, the humour in this particular situation could only be explained in terms of a rook and gull equation, the gulls in this instance being the bride's family who were being had with the tacit approval of everyone else.

So far as this individual was concerned, therefore, in making this joke this woman's feelings were of no account: by marrying, she had moved outside the pale of having any feelings at all in this, to him, very normal state of affairs. What is more, he assumed that her husband (whom he hadn't met for almost ten years) shared his system of values and sense of humour.

The ordeal of getting a girl married off has acquired grotesque dimensions in Indian society. Female foeticide/infanticide are among its most tragic manifestations. If the girl survives either of these fates, other horrors await her. The more bizarre consequences of this continuance of a rapacious practice are seen in the suicide of the three young sisters in Kanpur, Uttar Pradesh, who hanged themselves to escape the misery and humiliation of being born into a family which could not afford to provide them with suitable dowries. They are also seen in the 'sale' of innumerable young Muslim girls to aged Arab visitors who sexually exploit and then abandon them.

What is disturbing is that it is assumed by and large, in such circumstances, that a parent's act may be condoned, whatever the circumstances, since it takes place within an allegedly unchangeable sociocultural context. During a discussion I had with three 'educated' Indian men on the Arab issue mentioned above, I found all three surprisingly adamant about the girl's father having had no choice in the matter. Ergo, he was helpless and could not be condemned. The money the Arab bridegroom paid him was obviously something he needed badly. It was even argued that I could not be expected to appreciate his action or his reasons for it because I had never experienced a similar situation of economic deprivation.

I asked one of these men whether, knowing what might lie in store for his daughter after marriage, the money the father got didn't seem too high a price to pay for his daughter's alleged happiness and security. Apparently, that was not his problem! He had done his duty as a father by marrying her off. In the process, I was further told, he had also discharged his duty to his other dependants by doing well out of the marriage. His responsibility was to see his daughter married: what happened to her after marriage was something he could not expect to control.

How could the father's responsibility not encompass his daughter's subsequent unhappiness, especially if he willingly and knowingly contributed to it by forcibly giving her away in a marriage which he knew was likely to cause her only misery? Further, even if his was an unfortunate, impoverished, hopeless position, had he any right as a father to try and improve it by condemning his daughter to certain unhappiness? Was his daughter so dispensable?

I imagine that most people would maintain that this is in fact so in India, that daughters are often all too dispensable. They would even argue, in unambiguous terms, like the men referred to above, that such dispensability is right and justifiable. Such a framework of values, which is well-defined if somewhat questionable, would not be very different from the rationale provided in many women-related matters by the orthodox traditionalists (or distorters of tradition). However, it should not in these circumstances be mixed up with dubious arguments about context or need, or how one would have to be in that particular situation to appreciate a father's compulsions.

The 'situation' itself is clearly spelt out in the case of eleven-year-old Ameena of Hyderabad, who sprang into notoriety when an air-hostess spotted her on board an Indian Airlines flight. Inquiries revealed that Ameena had been married off to a *fifty-seven-year-old* Arab national and that she was unhappy and unwilling to accompany him. Ameena was rescued by the air-hostess, but the protracted legal battle which followed has hardly been encouraging. In the first instance, the air-hostess was denied adoption rights on the grounds that she was single. Second, Ameena's own future seems distinctly bleak. She may have become something of a cause célèbre, but that seems irrelevant to the options open to her. Her parents are defiant and sullen and see the publicity as a phenomenon they could have done without: it has damaged *their* image in the community.

Anees Jung's 'Little girls down the lane' (*Times of India*, 19 July 1992) outlines some of the problems involved in the rehabilitation of girls like Ameena. Specific among these is the official aftermath of such incidents along with their lack of meaningful significance so far as the victims themselves are concerned. Following on the public outrage, a process of educating these girls has been initiated by the government. However, the fact that sixteen hundred young Muslim girls are becoming literate because of Ameena means very little to her, and in no way amends the destruction of all her hopes and dreams.

Moreover, given the kind of response described earlier, from educated Indians who pleaded for a *contextual* understanding of the Ameena case, it is doubtful whether all the publicity will prove an effective deterrent to recurrences of such incidents. Anees Jung's article makes it clear that, whatever the 'reasons' for this sale of young girls to rich Arabs, the phenomenon cannot be shrugged off if we are to ameliorate the shame of its innumerable victims, all of them married off because of extreme poverty: Afzal Begum, married at fourteen to a sixty-two-year-old Arab who actually *chose* her in preference to her elder sister who was to have been the bride, took her to a hotel, did 'everything', and disappeared from her life a few days later; Naseem who was abandoned after two months though she was pregnant; and so on.

It hardly comes as a surprise that both Afzal Begum and Naseem are adamant about not wanting to marry again. Yet, in our sort of world, they would even be regarded as relatively more fortunate because they are both at vocational centres where they are learning, hopefully, to stand on their own feet. What price such independence, one might well say, except that Ameena's father won't even permit her to go to one of these. According to her mother, 'It is a question of his izzat.'

So once again, we return to the dubious connotations of the word 'izzat'. Various responses to what honour means exist in different cultures. In one of the more flamboyant of these, Shakespeare's memorable character Falstaff had rhetorically dismissed honour as 'a mere word' (*Henry IV, Part One*). However, it is doubtful whether even a Falstaff could have visualized the enormous tragic ramifications the word would acquire in conservative worlds, or for the Ameenas of twentieth century India.

The three daughters mentioned earlier in this chapter hanged themselves because they were unwilling to survive in such a system or to see their father humiliated on their behalf. Like the girls who were sold to affluent Arabs, they paid the price for living in an unfair world where their worth was determined by their father's financial status. Unlike Ameena or Afzal Begum they made their own, fatal choice: they opted out of the system while they were able to. They chose death rather than a fate *literally* worse than death. In fact it may be only a short while before *their* sacrifice is glorified in the way the actions of the Rajput queens who immolated themselves have been. For both, by travelling along different paths, arrived at the same end (i.e. deliberate suicide) and achieved it with the same ostensible intent, viz. the preservation of izzat. The only difference in this instance is that the act has jolted our modern sensibilities, albeit superficially and temporarily.

If one were to analyse what their sad fate implies, there

would be several differing views. As already mentioned, there are some people who would argue that we should not judge such events too harshly but in proper perspective. Such a view would, in other words, rationalize both the continuing folly of the fathers of daughters on the one hand, and the society that condones, even promotes, such folly on the other. Few of the 'general' public would regard the situation as unnatural and *not* unchangeable, a system that needs to be attacked and eradicated through consciousness-raising and concerted opposition. As long as the practice of dowry is thus rationalized, in terms of a world-order that we should rather be denying and opposing, the problem will remain an insoluble one. This is obvious from the way in which comparatively more enlightened practices, like the gifting of strīdhana, are abused with impunity.

Strīdhana literally means a woman's property. The term is used in common parlance to refer to the property (jewellery and gifts) given to a daughter by her parents when she marries. Kane (p.770) refers to the wedding hymn in the *Ṛg. Veda* (X.85.13,38) where bridal gifts are mentioned. The reference given here and from other sources indicate that these were gifts meant for the bride, in order to please her. The *Taittirīya Saṁhitā,* VI.2.1.1 tells us that 'the wife [of the sacrificer] holds on [to the cart], for the wife is the mistress of the household gear' (Kane, p. 770). 'And those deluded relatives who live off a woman's property—her carriages, her clothes, and so on—are evil and go to hell' (*Manu 3.52,* p. 48).

Kane (p. 777) also refers to Devala and Manu. Devala is quoted as saying that the different forms of strīdhana are for the woman alone; the husband cannot lay claim to them except in times of distress. Manu (9.200) warns that the husband's heirs, if they divide the ornaments worn by a woman during her husband's lifetime, incur a sin. This is a dubious pronouncement in the first instance, but what is significant is that it is one which is happily ignored in the more grisly operations of patriarchal orthodoxy. It is not uncommon to find a woman's ornaments appropriated by her rapacious in-laws, and worn with no ostensible sense of fear or shame. There are variations on these interpretations. By and large, however, they conclude that a woman had absolute authority over her strīdhana. (For a more detailed study, see Sindhu S. Dange, 'Some aspects of Woman's Property (Strīdhana)—A Rethinking', in *New Horizons of Research in Indology,* Silver Jubilee Volume, ed. V. N. Jha, Centre of Advanced Study in Sanskrit, Pune, 1989, pp. 158–65.)

It is clear that the debasement of this practice into 'dowry' developed even as strīdhana continued to be given. Moreover, this parallel development has repeatedly blurred the real intent of strīdhana. In a letter written to *Femina's* legal columnist (23 July 1994), an anguished 'twenty-nine-year-old, well-qualified Gujarati girl' recounts the wily manoeuvres by means of which her strīdhana has been appropriated by her alcoholic husband's family. Ironically, the woman's father-in-law is an 'eminent social activist in Ahmedabad'.

Though the attorney's advice suggests that the woman could seek and obtain legal action against her husband and his family, it is clear that the battle will be a long one and that it would involve enormous financial expense without guaranteeing any success. What is even more distressing is the fact that such an incident is only the tip of the iceberg, a case involving a woman who is articulate and presumably in a position to fight this battle. The more common experience would be the multiplication, *ad infinitum*, of similar incidents, with the woman either in no position to resist or conditioned to accept what has happened as God-given because of her gender. It is conveniently overlooked here that the very sanctions which liken a woman's husband to her god also forbid him access to her property. But this is the androcentric code of paradoxes which ultimately exists to promote the exploitation of a woman, frequently by her own sex.

Chapter 6

Wife and Mother

> About three weeks after we were married, one of my husband's colleagues invited us to dinner. Among those present that evening was another man who worked in the same place, a bachelor whose mother-tongue was the same as my husband's. On learning that my husband had spent a year in Italy recently, he asked him whether it was true that Italian girls were very good in bed. When my husband said he didn't know, Bachelor Boy wouldn't believe him. He dug my husband in the ribs, saying he shouldn't be afraid to tell the truth because they were talking together in Bengali, a language I didn't understand then!
>
> (An incident narrated by a woman I know).

Is one being hypersensitive in finding such a story offensive? Most male Indians would probably say yes. It may even be pointed out that many men abroad continue to have their peccadilloes with their wives being none the wiser. The difference here, however, is that the wife was actually present when her husband's sexual adventures (real or alleged) were sought to be discussed in a language she didn't know, while the stand taken implied that sexual experience was a male prerogative. It could be explored, dissected, and mulled over with infinite enjoyment by men as long as the wife didn't know.

Moreover, here, as in most similar instances, the assumption was clearly sexist. Bachelor Boy could have been excused his puerile wit only if he could be seen as operating within a scale of values which, however dubious one may be about them, granted the same kind of licence to women. It is hard to imagine however that he would have even dreamed of directing a similar query to the man's wife about *her* possible experiences during her years abroad.

What is equally likely is that if *she* had volunteered to elaborate on the theme of her sexual exploits (assuming of course that there was scope for elaboration or that she would have cared to do so if there was), he and the rest of those present would undoubtedly have found these less than funny. They would have labeled her a whore and wondered how her husband could have endured the agony of discovering how debased she was. They may even have held her up as an archetype of the kind of woman Manu had had in mind in advocating the need for licentious womankind to be kept under strict control at all times.

Like the incident concerning dowry, mentioned in the earlier chapter, this one bothers me. Taken together, they seem to constitute a framework of tacit understanding about the nature and function of marriage. In both, a woman's feelings are seen as dispensable. In the second instance, it is clearly stated that what a wife won't know can't hurt her: ergo, deception is all right and is, in fact, an accepted male way of living life to the lees.

Writing of the married woman in the 1950s, Simone de Beauvoir had observed that she was expected to have sexual pleasure only in a specific role, i.e. as wife. Sexual intercourse was thus reduced to an institution. But while this was binding on a woman, denying her sexual desire or gratification outside marriage, a man's public role as worker and citizen made it possible for him to 'enjoy contingent pleasures before marriage and extramaritally' (*The Second Sex,* pp. 454–55).

Female sexuality in the West over the past forty years has, however, become a more acknowledged, if not entirely approved, facet of a woman's existence (even Bachelor Boy's remarks about Italian girls would make that clear). In contrast, except for instances so isolated that they may be viewed as marginal and largely superfluous, there has been no overt change in the Indian attitude to sex and the Indian woman. Moreover, since 'arranged marriages' remain the rule, the possibilities for the manifestation of female sexuality remain by and large insignificant. Female virginity is still imperative in an arranged marriage.

'A virtuous wife should constantly serve her husband like a god, *even if he behaves badly, freely indulges his lust, and is devoid of any good qualities*' (*Manu,* 5.154, p. 115, italics mine). It would appear that the Śāstras acknowledged the aberrations of men and even listed those forms of adultery which were socially acceptable. Nārada[1] (*Strīpuṁsa*, 78–79) states that intercourse was permitted with prostitutes or slaves, provided they were of a lower caste! (Kane, p. 638). The 'Ādiparva' of the *Mahābhārata* (115.39) narrates how Dhṛtarāṣṭra was entertained by a courtesan when his wife Gāndharī was pregnant (Kane, p. 637). Since Gāndharī is also commonly acknowledged as having been a pativratā of the highest order,[2] there is a sad irony in the fact that this deviation in Dhṛtarāṣṭra does not give rise to any censure.

According to *Yājñavalkya II,* there were two kinds of concubines. The avaruddha was one who actually lived in the same house but was forbidden to have intercourse with any other male, while the bhujiṣyā was a woman who was kept elsewhere (not in the house) and was further the exclusive preserve of the man who kept her.

The matter-of-fact manner in which these types are differentiated, along with the strictures regarding different sorts of courtesans or prostitutes, is the more remarkable because of the strict code of conduct imposed on women.

'A woman who is unfaithful to her husband is an object of reproach in this world; [then] she is reborn in the womb of a jackal and is tormented by the diseases born of her evil' (*Manu,* 5.164, p. 116).

The smṛtis even provided for the maintenance of these concubines. This may be interpreted at one level as a humane measure since the woman, whether as wife or concubine, was more often than not a victim. At the same time, there is more than a suggestion of double standards in such acceptance of a man's right to legitimately enjoy the services of a woman other than his wife.

The relevance of such codes to present-day Indian society has been discussed in the various chapters of this book. It is indisputable that they inform contemporary attitudes by providing a historical and sanctioned rationale for feudal assumptions regarding women. My father had a relative who openly 'kept' a woman of another, (lower!) caste and had several children by her. Their presence and paternity was commonly acknowledged. This sexual deviancy would never have been condoned in a *woman* from my father's family.

The broad significance of such an attitude is sufficiently embedded in the present-day Indian consciousness to affect our perception of the duties of husband and wife. For instance, the fact that Indian marriages are by and large more 'stable' than those in Western societies is self-righteously explained by reference to the rigid codes circumscribing our social lives and practices: these are therefore seen as both justified and desirable. It is ignored that what passes for a stable (i.e. unbroken) marriage may often be a choice without alternatives. Similarly, the fact that marriages are breaking up even in India indicates not so much what the conservatives would see as our 'corruption' by Western values but that more and more women are asserting their rights within marriage.

Simone de Beauvoir had commented on the thankless nature of most housework, and had even compared it to the 'torture of Sisyphus'. Its 'endless repetition' had seemed futile, a mere perpetuation of the housewife's uneventful existence (*The Second Sex*, p. 470). Unacknowledged martyrdom has always been part of a housewife's existence. Like housewives the world over, the Indian housewife has always been expected to subordinate her own needs to those of her family. However, while the sort of drudgery described by de Beauvoir is restricted to physical slavery, the Indian context with its vastly different tradition of family ties and commitments prescribes an all-encompassing bondage.

The Indian wife is often a martyr to not merely her husband's needs but those of his family as well. Moreover, while women in the West have attempted to consolidate themselves and struggle against forms of oppression implicit in being a wife, this has only made them examples of what stridharma would prohibit the ideal Indian wife from doing.

This response has an ideological basis in many modes of struggle against oppression, and it reveals the fundamentally reactionary vision of many revolutionaries as regards gender-related issues. bell hooks draws attention to the way in which black militants tried to suggest that more freedom for women was a *white* value which had to be avoided at all costs. She quotes from Amiri Bakara ('Black Women' in *Black World*, 1970) his view that 'We talk about the black woman and the black man like we were separate because we have been separated . . . .'

Bakara calls upon all blacks to erase this separateness by asserting their African identities, i.e. by 'embracing a value system that knows of no separation but only of the divine complement the black woman is for her man.' Insisting that the concept of equality of men and women is the invention of the 'devils and the devilishly influenced', Bakara says that such equality goes against nature. The black 'brother', according to Bakara, would prefer a woman to be a woman and a man to 'be a ma-an' (*Ain't I a Woman: Black Women and Feminism,* p. 95).

While it is true that the larger Indian world-outlook denies even men a wholly independent, individualistic identity (I return to this theme in my concluding chapter), a woman is even further constrained by virtue of her total dependence on her husband within the prescribed rituals of existence: 'Apart from their [husbands], women cannot sacrifice or undertake a vow or fast . . . ' (*Manu,* 5.155, p. 115). She therefore passes effortlessly from her father's possession into her husband's.

In the Gita, Kṛṣṇa advises Arjuna to perform his duty to the best of his ability and to remain indifferent to the fruits of his labour. Like many seemingly sound philosophical statements, this one has a progressive and a regressive side to it. On the negative side, this could be a self-perpuating rationale for the social stasis of repressed groups such as women. At any rate, these lines, which have acquired a seminal status in the Hindu view of life, are remarkably suited to the role of the ideal wife. More often than not, hers is a thankless round of service demanded and unacknowledged. In innumerable urban middle-class homes even today, husbands expect their wives to fetch and carry just about everything, from a glass of water to their shoes and socks.

The 'Letters' columns of popular women's magazines like *Femina* present an interesting collage of the problems and insecurities faced by middle-class teenaged girls and young women in India. To some extent, these are also representative of the pattern of life in Indian society. I take two such letters from the 8 July 1992 issue as examples.

The first of these is from a nineteen-year-old who has had a sexual relationship with a boy she loves and who she says loves her. Their marriage, however, seems impossible because, according to her, she would never be accepted by his parents who were close family friends and saw her as a sister to the boy rather than as his future wife.

The second letter is written by a newly-married woman

who was brought up as a strict vegetarian but has been married into a family which is 'strictly non-vegetarian' (!). Though allowed to continue as a vegetarian she has to help in preparing the meals and finds the prospect so revolting that she has stopped entering the kitchen. She is now afraid that her in-laws 'whom I really respect very much, may think I'm a lazy, good-for-nothing "bahu".'

The first letter contains an all-too familiar theme. Whatever the degree of friendship or intimacy between boys and girls, marriage is commonly regarded as a family affair and family decisions in this respect are usually regarded as sacrosanct. It is the second letter, however, which makes two very interesting points.

The first of these, by inference, is that the writer cannot speak to her in-laws about this very mundane matter; the second is that her inability to explain her true feelings may result in a gross misunderstanding about her qualities as a daughter-in-law. Both these points assume even more significance in the context of the very large number of similar letters which appear in such columns. Their recurrence would suggest that none of the women who write them have any alternative except the pathetic solace of a lonely-hearts column. Such a scenario reflects the melodrama and occasional tragedy of our so-called perfect marriage-syndrome.

Both letters are also rooted in our traditional expectation that the girl a man marries takes on service to his family as one of her primary duties. On the positive side, such an attitude reinforces the community-bonding which is one of the distinguishing features of our social existence. On the negative side however, are the extremes generally incorporated within this notion of service.

Yājñavalkya (I.83 and 87) says that besides keeping the house running smoothly and giving in to a husband's demands, a wife should show respect to her parents-in-law by clasping their feet. The *Viṣṇu Dharma Sūtra,*[3] 25.1–6, asserts that the wife should honour 'the mother-in-law, the father-in-law, other elders, gods, guests and keep the household utensils well arranged.' Bṛhaspati, whose definition of the pativratā has been quoted in Chapter 1, says that a wife should arise before her husband and elders and eat only after they have eaten. She should occupy a seat lower than that of the husband or elders. In Vanaparva,[4] chapter 233, Draupadī is made to declare that she avoids whatever her husband does not eat, drink, or partake of (Kane, pp. 563–65). This particular form of abstinence is still regarded as evidence of devotion and service in marriage.

The continued exaltation of such self-effacing norms makes for a form of emotional blackmail which is used to pressurize the girl/woman/wife who would like to resist them. She is seen as a house-breaker, someone who drives a wedge between her husband and his family. It is hardly ever acknowledged that a man's loyalties would naturally shift or at least become more than parent-focussed after marriage. Anxious, therefore, to avoid the charge that they have spoilt the girl or brought her up badly, her parents begin moulding her from girlhood in the role she would be called upon to play.

Engaged, she moves towards a more specific aim: to approximate the ideal wife. If she performs this role well, she is exalted and praised even by men with allegedly radical views. I have frequently heard such men describe women in the following way: 'She may not be particularly intelligent or interesting but she obviously makes a good wife.' The condescending flavour of such remarks, the implication that being a 'good wife' is the one quality a woman ought not to lack, limits the range of a man-woman relationship in marriage.

Bṛhaspati's code for the way an ideal wife should conduct herself in her husband's home is still largely accepted and observed. As already pointed out (Chapter 2), the Śāstras sanctified the quality of self-denial in a wife. Even in fairly progressive homes of my mother's generation, the woman was generally expected to serve the guests and the rest of the household, eating only after they had finished. Given the Indian method of cooking and serving, where no definite portions are allocated as an individual's share, this could mean that the more delicious dishes were often consumed by the others before she had sat down to her meal.

This practice continues in many homes even today. I have been frequently embarrassed because I have asked the hostess to join us, only to be told that she would eat only after her husband had had his meal! Embarrassed because I was never sure, in such a situation, as to what my act of doing so must imply and yet unable to bring myself to say, 'OK, in that case I'll stop eating too, and we can both eat together later.'

The orthodox Indian view interprets any resistance to its androcentric codes as being the influence of Western decadence. We continue to cling to forms of female oppression, exalting and glorifying them with practised rhetoric. I have already referred, in Chapter 3, to the manner in which Mr K. R. Malkani had reviled critics who feared that the party was anti-women. Malkani was clearly upholding the same sort of ideology which bell hooks has accused black militants like Amir Bakara of espousing. Both Bakara and Malkani are essentially misusing emotive issues such as colonialism and racism to assert a set of values which are allegedly native to a community's culture but which in effect are damaging to the interests and liberation of women.

Hitler's promise to return women to 'Kinder, Kűche, Kirche' ('Children, Cooking, Church') had a similar appeal to conservative forces in Germany's social life. Like nearly all reactionary interpretations have done, Hitler's too saw a woman's world as consisting of 'her husband, her family, her children, and her home'. In a stance that is remarkably similar to Amir Bakara's, Hitler had argued that it was false to state that respect called for 'the overlapping of the spheres of activity of the sexes'. Rather, it demanded that 'neither sex should try to do that which belongs to the other' (from Hitler's speech to the National Socialist Women's Organization, September 1934. Quoted by Gloria Steinem in *Outrageous Acts and Everyday Rebellions,* p. 319: 'If Hitler Were Alive, Whose Side Would He Be On?').

The enormous research carried out by feminists into the lives of women over the past few centuries has revealed that, whatever the religio-cultural framework, a certain common patriarchal ethic sought to relegate women to secondary roles. The increasing exclusion of women from the public sphere was subtly achieved by buttressing such exclusion with seductive images of the alleged essence of womanhood. Implicit in all these was the virtue of self-denial, indeed of self-obliteration.

In this evolutionary process, one category which becomes a common, acceptable, non-offending global denominator for all women is the category of motherhood. Adrienne Rich has analysed in sensitive detail the growth of the institution of motherhood, and the modes in which this has influenced the individual woman's perception of the experience (*Of Woman Born: Motherhood as Experience and Institution.* W.W. Norton and Company, New York, 1976, Foreword, p. xi).

In an equally insightful examination of motherhood, Elizabeth Fox-Genovese comments of how, during the Enlightenment,[5] 'in a surprisingly brief span of time', the Judaeo-Christian world which had long seen women as inherently evil began to see them as essentially good. Women were however identified in terms of their specific relations with the men within families: as 'mothers, wives, and daughters' (*Feminism Without Illusions: A Critique of Individualism*, p. 124). This predominant world-view also informs the late eighteenth century writer Mary Wollstonecraft's insistence that if men would but allow themselves to enjoy the benefits of 'rational fellowship' with women rather than expecting 'slavish obedience' from them, they would 'find us more observant daughters, more affectionate sisters, more faithful wives, more reasonable mothers—in a word, better citizens.' ('A Vindication of the Rights of Woman', 1792. This extract is taken from *Woman as Revolutionary*, edited by Frederick C. Giffon, Mentor, 1973, pp. 56–7.)

As Fox-Genovese further points out, of the three roles listed above, that of the mother came to be unquestionably preferred. It enabled the minimizing of female sexuality and promoted the idea of woman as primarily devoted to the nurture of men. Motherhood 'became the reigning sign of the submission of the female self to the make individual' (p. 125).

Fox-Genovese sees the eighteenth century as having crystallized 'the ideal of motherhood . . . as woman's highest mission—as her distinct career', even though there were earlier precedents (p. 124). In the Indian context, with its rootedness in tradition as the informing force in social practice, motherhood has long been a category which is emphasized, a role which the girl-child is conditioned to accept as the end she has been created for. As already indicated (Chapter 3), a man married to beget sons, a purpose which even today single-mindedly determines a woman's status as wife and mother.

Motherhood in India is further merged with a multi-layered pattern of societal relationships to which a woman is expected to conform. No matter what community she belongs to, she usually performs the triple role of daughter-in-law, wife and mother. The nuclear family is a recent urban phenomenon, and housing conditions in the metropolitan cities are making it increasingly difficult for this new phenomenon to survive. Many young couples are forced to either move in with their parents (very often resulting in the sort of pressures consequent upon living together in cramped conditions) or depend on them substantially for help with the children, especially if both husband and wife happen to hold jobs.

Even otherwise, the family web is usually binding and inescapable. The ties between one generation and the next are still very powerful, whether for emotional or other, socially imposed, reasons. Such closeness has its strength as well as limitations. The strengths are implicit in the sense of bonding, fraternity, social duty, responsibility towards the old and the helpless, all of which the Śāstras do contain in a very large measure. This sense of community, characteristic of our social/family existence, is unlike the individualistic mode of family life in the West. In India, a break with the family structure is still more or less impossible. Where it does exist, it is anything but representative of Indian social life.

Yet, in both the Western and the Indian context, and indeed globally, motherhood implies a loss of individual freedom. Virginia Woolf, writing in the early part of the twentieth century, had described the archetypal endowments of what she termed the 'Angel of the House'. She was 'intensely sympathetic, . . . immensely charming . . . utterly unselfish, . . . sacrificed herself daily' (*Feminist Literary Theory, A Reader,* Basil Blackwell, 1986, p. 52). Fox-Genovese has argued that the new concept of motherhood 'confirmed the new centrality of the individual, although not by endowing mothers with individualism. The purpose of motherhood was, rather, to nurture the individual' (p. 125). Both Simone de Beauvoir and Adrienne Rich have examined in some detail the negative emotions motherhood can arouse as well as their harmful manifestations because women have been conditioned to regard these as wrong and to feel guilty about them.

One of the finest contemporary depictions of Indian motherhood is the found in a poem, 'Of Mothers, Among Other Things', by the Indian English poet A. K. Ramanujan. With a total absence of sentimentality, Ramanujan in this poem constructs a characteristic, easily recognizable image of a woman whose life has been given to drudgery and self-negation. Her hands, wrinkled with housework, are like 'a wet eagle's/ two black pink-crinkled feet'. Her saris 'do not cling: they hang, loose feather of a onetime wing.' His mother is wholly unlike the voluptuously seductive women of traditional Indian art.

While the West may also project motherhood as signifying the absence of individual freedom, in India, as I argue in my concluding chapter, such freedom is in any case limited for men as well as women. Both function within a code which stresses the family and community. In the woman's case, such absence of individual freedom is overwhelming. Basically, a woman is answerable to a series of relationships on her husband's side. Decisions are usually collective, and it is assumed that this is for the good of all those involved.

The way in which this assumption influences individual behaviour may be seen in Rama Mehta's *Inside the Haveli*. Here the protagonist Gita keeps hoping that her husband would find a job in another university, perhaps Delhi, so that they could escape the stranglehold of the haveli. We are told that though Ajay, her husband, is aware of her unhappiness and himself finds the haveli oppressive, he is 'not prepared to do anything to challenge his father's authority' because he 'admired and respected' him (p. 19).

Implicit in this statement is the very Indian notion that respect for one's elders involves an unquestioning surrender to their views or wishes. Our traditional world-view of respect as constituting an irrational acceptance of practices, even if they seem wrong, unjust or meaningless, is hardly the most attractive feature of our relationships with our elders and with one another. There is, after all, an area of mutual respect and encounter where the exchange of differing ideas ought to be seen as acceptable and even welcomed. Moreover, whether she intends to or not, Mehta appears to condone a form of patriarchal absolutism, contained in the phrase 'challenge his father's authority'.

In such a system, the daughter-in-law's role is at best a passive one, aimed at doing what is expected of her and keeping the family, if not happy, then at least in no real position to find fault. The kind of back-breaking drudgery this could involve may be gauged from the fact that the average Indian housewife lacks even the basic time-saving household gadgets seen as essential by her Western counterpart. She goes through a daily *manual* routine of washing, cooking, grinding spices, shopping for groceries and vegetables in several different places where she may have to queue up to be served, caring for kids of varying ages, and serving her husband his tea and dinner when he returns home to relax, poor chap, after the rigours of his day *at work*. The archetypal (average) Indian male is not given to worrying his head about the trivia of domestic routine. It is expected that the woman would uncomplainingly take care of these even if she has another full-time job outside the home.

In a typical Indian home, children are seen as the mother's responsibility. The father does his bit by working to support the family, a blessed status which the entry of women into the work-force has done nothing to erode. The official emphasis on family planning has had a partial impact on the number of children a woman is compelled to bear. Even so, the rigours of running the home in the absence of an appropriate infrastructure sap the woman of a great deal of her vitality.

In a poem entitled 'Obstacle', Marathi poet Indira Sant refers to the total absorption of the household with the husband's life. The cook, servant, chauffeur and accountant never slip up in their knowledge of his likes, dislikes, routines, arrivals and exits. Even the children's letters, which arrive from abroad, are full of queries about *his* blood pressure, *his* travels, *his* doings: only the last line mentions the mother, a cursory message of respect, the conventional namaskar which ends every letter written in an Indian language. While the large domestic retinue of servants mentioned in the poem is far from characteristic of today's India, the preoccupation with the man's world is.

The mother in the Ramanujan poem referred to earlier is not the goddess of Hindu culture but a tired, shabby woman rushed off her feet by the demands of domesticity. The compassion in Ramanujan's description does not soften the unattractive reality of this woman with her shapeless saris and work-roughened fingers, so unlike the Sītās and Draupadīs of our television screens or the bahus and mas of our celluloid world. Yet, she is more typically 'mata'. Shorn of all the rhetoric, she is what the system has made her: she represents security, selflessness, oppression and, above all, silence.

The codes that have fashioned her are both dogmatic and contradictory. Manu said that while the teacher was more important than ten instructors, the father more than a hundred teachers, the mother was more important than a thousand fathers (2.145). The mother was likened to the physical form of one's own self: by loving and serving her, the householder could win this world (2.226, 233).

In spite of these exhortations to which lip-service is paid even today, the mother has clearly become a doormat in most homes. Her natural affection and desire to nurture and protect her brood is transformed into an exaggerated image of subserviency and martyrdom. She is the type glorified in a hundred different ways on the big screen and the small one. She is the wonder woman of the new commercials. She is Lalitaji, determined to stretch the budget and use money judiciously by opting for Surf from among all the detergents available; she smilingly washes her daughter's grubby dress in a Videocon washing-machine and waves her off to a party; she uses her skill as a Bharata Natyam dancer to demonstrate the virtues of a new washing-machine; she smears Vicks Vaporub on her child's nose and chest; she calls her family in to breakfast/ lunch/ dinner and surprises them with the magic of Dalda/ Amul Ghee/ a new dairy milk whitener; she shudders involuntarily when her daughter's would-be parents-in-law say they have just one more demand before the marriage ceremonies could begin and smiles coyly when it turns out to be something her lord and master has ready in his pocket: paan masala.

She is also the *Ma* found in innumerable regional films. She may be widowed young. She then endures all manner of hardships, puts up with varying forms of humiliation, and perseveres in her attempt to rear her children with dignity and a sound code of moral values. She may be exploited in various other ways. She may have a drunken husband who beats her with sickening regularity, or a lecherous employer who tries to molest her, but her message is clear.

She represents Indian womanhood. In other words, exploitation, suffering, sacrifice, all these are her lot. She bears them with fortitude and will on no account permit her children to seek revenge. The merest hint that this may happen, and she becomes a wrathful goddess. She is the oasis that never dries up in a world of arid deprivation and want. Like the woman in the television commercial referred to in Chapter 2, she would gladly forgo everything: heavily pregnant, she gives plentifully to her husband and son (not daughter), and smilingly holds up two dry rotis as proof that she won't starve.

It may appear as if I am being merely sceptical about the mother's role. While admitting that there are undeniable urges that make some mothers seem almost superhuman, I am dubious about the insistence on these being essential, a necessary prerequisite to good motherhood.

In the essay 'Erotica versus Pornography', Steinem has maintained that some male primates carry and generally 'mother' their infants. Male lions care for their young, while male penguins do virtually everything except child-bearing: they even hatch the eggs and sacrifice their own membranes to feed the new arrivals. Steinem surmises that this is probably why many male supremacists prefer to focus on male-dominant groups like chimps and baboons, and even these are usually studied in 'atypical conditions of captivity'. She concludes that this is part of an attempt to project a highly distorted message, viz. that human females should accept sex as part of an 'animal destiny' and see child-bearing and child-rearing as inseparable (*Outrageous Acts and Everyday Rebellions*, p. 224).

Steinem's scepticism about motherhood as female destiny, as essence of femaleness, finds an echo in Adrienne Rich's study of it as experience and institution. Rich's thesis has a substantial interlocking of emotion and logic and is a valuable examination of one of the most mystified and misinterpreted roles in the history of civilization. While I may not accept her arguments in toto, I have reservations about those codes in my own culture which demand that a mother be like a goddess.

The Indian mother is no divine being. She is human and has the same basic animal instincts and desires that her male counterpart is allowed to have. She too may desire good food, the first serving, the best portions. She wants to call it a day sometimes, to be free of the endless clamour. She wants peace, quiet, the ability occasionally to be selfish, to gobble up the ice cream her child is shrilly demanding. But in our Śāstra-ridden psyches, the pativratā is willy-nilly conditioned into sublimating a whole series of natural urges, or at least believing that she should endeavour to do so.

Sheila Rowbotham has drawn attention to 'the mystique of ideal mothering and the exhaustion of actual mothering' (*The Past Is Before Us*, Beacon Press, 1989, p. 33). Yet, given the far more individualistic lifestyle of the West, there is at least the theoretical possibility of individual choices. In our community-centred existence, such choices are virtually inconceivable for the most part.

An Indian friend living in the US told me recently that her paediatrician believed that if women fed themselves before they fed their children there would be a healthier atmosphere at meal-times. His advice was realistic, sensible and, for a man, unusual. However, this mode of action was more easily recommended than implemented. My friend came up against a barrage of recriminations from her mother-in-law who, widowed young, had brought up her children with archetypal fortitude and had in the process acquired a very virtuous, self-righteous stance about Indian women and their strīdharma. Not surprisingly, she saw the paediatrician's advice as 'foreign to our *saṅskṛti*'.[6] It had to be something to do with 'those foreign women. No wonder there are so many divorces in this country! *I* never did this to any of my children. Nor, I'm sure, did your mother, or any of the mothers I've seen back in India. You may be Indian, but you think like an American.'

The rest of the evening was a never-ending series of accusations and denials, at the end of which my friend failed to convince anyone that the doctor had had a point. In the interests of peace, therefore, she reverted to the earlier pattern—at least while her mother-in-law was with her. She had the option of seeing the compromise as only a temporary one. Many Indian women don't.

Why are Indian women so manifestly hostile to one another, especially in relationships where they could, through mutual bonding, achieve so much? Part of the answer may be that the mother, because of her confinement within the house and her inability to develop and grow except in home-and-children related roles, ends up surrendering to the traditional clap-trap about the mother as goddess. Mythicizing her role gives her a degree of fulfilment in life. This self-deception also perpetuates the power-equations whereby the woman/mother eventually sees her imprisonment as empowering her by conferring on her the attributes of mother and wife. She sees these largely (perhaps naturally) in relation to the men in the domestic power-hierarchy (husband/sons). She thus becomes a symbol of what men later on expect their women to be. She is imprinted on the children's consciousness as sublime sufferer, selfless slave, tireless worker for her family's comfort and happiness.

At the same time, she perpetuates the injustice shown to her as woman by making her preference clear: she desires sons, not daughters. It is on her son that she focuses all her obsessive love and yearning. He becomes the object of her future hopes and dreams. She makes him grow up convinced that he is someone special and that he should expect the woman/women in his life to feel the same.

When her son reaches a 'marriageable' age, his family acquires a special aura. At other weddings, the parents of young girls eye him speculatively. The proposals begin to pour in, generally accompanied by photographs and horoscopes. Infinite variety, which the family pores over for days on end. Then come the visits to the girl's home or, if the families are 'modern', a meeting arranged through a mutual acquaintance. And all the while, the girl is scrutinized like a prize heifer to be selected or rejected.

The humiliating process over, the girl eventually marries and enters her new home, only to find herself regarded as an intruder whom the mother-in-law sees as a threat to her carefully nurtured relationship with her son (now the girl's husband). Unless enlightened and rational to an almost suprahuman degree, the mother jealously guards against any evidence that her power vis-à-vis her son is weakening. Moreover, complex knots bind most Indian men to their mothers. The rationale for these may be found in the smrtis. P. V. Kane (Vol.II, p. 580) cites several examples which, taken in sum, ascribe a significant and prominent position to the mother. They are commonly agreed that a mother has special claims on her son and that he should never abandon her. According to Kane, the *Śaṅkha-Likhita*[7] even advocates that, while a son should normally not intervene in a quarrel between his parents he should, if he chooses to, side with the mother because she has borne and nourished him.

Her son's marriage signals the start of an ongoing battle between the mother and her daughter-in-law. Common experience suggests that it is mothers who, especially as mothers-in-law, impose impossible norms of good-wifeliness even when there is no evidence of explicit ill-treatment. Since even the proverbial worm will turn, there comes a day when the mother-in-law, through age and/or widowhood, is reduced to a position of impotence and is herself a target of another woman's frustration. The once young bride is now poised for her big role: mother and, eventually, mother-in-law.

Chapter 7

Post-Script

> There is no magic left in man-woman relationships any more. Women these days are so forthright, so intimidating that it is hard to approach them, let alone think of marrying them.
>
> (View expressed by Ajit Mani, an unmarried advertising executive from Bangalore. 'A Matter of Loneliness', *The Indian Express, Sunday Magazine,* 23 August 1992).

In Chapter 1, I had referred to Makarand Paranjape's summing-up of the 'new woman': a 'selfish woman', she was unable to give of herself and only knew how to 'take-take-take' (*Femina*, 8 October 1992). The brief observation quoted above is in a similar vein. Both views are sceptical about the identity of those contemporary women who have redefined their roles and priorities. There is a frighteningly categorical flavour about both opinions which suggests that for these two men at any rate (and they may be regarded as broadly representing the Indian male view-point) the liberation of women in hardly an unqualified blessing.

Such scepticism is of course not confined to India. Susan Faludi's book, *Backlash*, which I have also mentioned earlier, makes it clear that there is an ongoing counter-resistance to the women's movement in America, which has assumed the proportions of what she terms an 'undeclared war'. Writing in the *Times Literary Supplement* of 25 June 1993, feminist critic and academic Elaine Showalter wryly remarks that readers (especially American readers) in the 1990s might well be led to believe that it is feminists, rather than other subversive forces like 'serial killers, religious fanatics, fascist arsonists, or terrorist bombers', who constitute the real threat to social peace and security ('Feminists under fire: Images of the New Woman from the Nineties to the 1990s').

Showalter refers to Republican Patrick Buchanan's condemnation of feminism: 'a socialist, anti-family political movement that encourages women to leave their husbands, kill their children, practise witchcraft, destroy capitalism, and become lesbians'. This far from wholesome view would appear to find an echo in other twentieth century contexts, ranging from Rebecca West's observation (1913) that people called her a feminist whenever she expressed sentiments that distinguished her from a doormat (Faludi, p. xxiii) to the blinkered diatribes of those who subscribed to the red scare of the McCarthy era in the 1950s.

Sara M. Evans quotes John Hanna, a Columbia University professor who maintained that girls' schools and women's colleges in the 1950s were infiltrated by 'some of the most loyal disciples of Russia'. The teachers in these institutions were described by him as 'frustrated females', whose bitter struggles had infected their personal attitudes with a 'political dogma based on hatred' (*Born for Liberty*, The Free Press, New York, Collier Macmillan Publishers, 1989, p. 244). In the 1970s, right-wing activist Phyllis Schlafly denounced the feminist magazine *Ms.* as being 'anti-family, anti-children, and pro-abortion' (Evans, p. 304).

It is not surprising that feminism continues to arouse hostility in a context so vastly different as the Indian one. Worse, misapprehensions about the purpose and nature of feminism can result in distorted statements made by even its alleged supporters. Such is fashion designer Hemant Trivedi's insistence that while *he* respects feminism, believes in equality, and considers that women are better-equipped to handle crises, 'every woman wants to be a sex symbol'. Women, according to this convert to feminism, come in 'five avatars': the girl-next door, the mother-figure, the dumb blonde, the sex symbol, and the cool, sophisticated career-oriented type ('Women Are Still Just Sex Symbols!', *Femina,* June 23, 1992)!

My emphasis on popular magazines like *Femina* is because these are by and large an accurate index to the popular consciousness, especially of the Indian middle class. While this is globally true to some extent, the importance of such magazines in the Indian context is determined by several factors such as the combined power, in a developing society, of élitism, the burgeoning bourgeoisie, and its desperate bid to acquire what it perceives as the discreet charms of the bourgeoisie elsewhere. In India this manifests itself in the manner in which these magazines become repositories of the dreams and aspirations of the middle classes. Reputations are built on the basis of having featured in them. They create social celebrities out of ordinary men and women, direct public taste and have an all-pervading sphere of influence. They are read in almost all middle-class homes.

At the same time, their outlook is generally conservative. In spite of a symbolic movement in the direction of more radical ideologies, they assert the fundamental values of 'Kinder, Küche, Kirche' (to borrow Hitler's phrase). This reluctance to incorporate more iconoclastic modes of thought in gender-related issues is present in the Indian media as a whole. In *Whose News? The Media and Women's Issues,* editors Ammu Joseph and Kalpana Sharma, both of whom have had considerable journalistic experience, refer to the selective process through which the media publicizes women's issues. They argue that the increasing efforts of the press to publicize various newsworthy issues are still conditioned by traditional notions of what constitutes 'news'. The manner in which women's issues are persistently sidelined suggests that 'what we would call the "feminization" of the news process has not yet taken place' (p. 32).

Traditional/conservative opinion would exalt the unprotesting woman, singling her out as an example of far greater resilience and inner strength. It is worth noting that in another context, that of the black woman's alleged strength in the face of victimization, bell hooks had pointed out that 'to be strong in the face of oppression is not the same as overcoming oppression . . . endurance is not to be confused with transformation' (*Ain't I A Woman: Black Women and Feminism*, South End Press, 1981, p. 6). Part of my effort in this book has been to try and extend this argument to counter the reluctance of the Indian intelligentsia to view feminism rationally.

Like any *–ism,* feminism may be described as composed of three facets: sociological, ideological, and moral/ethical. My basic concern has been with the first two of these. I see the third as linked to them, in that it would be concerned with such basic issues like the equality of the sexes and the essential goodness and desirability of such equality.

If one were to define feminism simply as the equality of the sexes, there would be fundamental problems arising out of the very concept of equality in social practice. In spite of the theoretical acceptance of the ideology of equality in human society, it becomes all too apparent that inequality has an unquestionable part to play in all human operations. Recognizing the paradoxes inherent in such a situation, bell hooks attempts to 'reappropriate the term "feminism", to focus on the fact that to be "feminist" in any authentic sense of the term is to want for all people, female and male, liberation from sexist role patterns, domination, and oppression' (*Ain't* . . . , p. 195).

Without even encompassing radical departures from

gender-roles, this would mean first of all that so-called traditional roles are relocated in the scale of public valuing. Thus, the symbolic change in terminology from *housewife* to *home-maker* could, if ideologically apprehended and defined, give housework a degree of professional importance. This does not of course mean that one is camouflaging the true nature of housework. Rather, that one is recognizing its value as *work*, its contribution to national productivity, its importance as something which goes beyond the conventional devaluing it as being of no consequence. While feminists abroad have made this an important item on their agenda, women in India still continue to function within an androcentric code which views domestic work as demeaning and best left to women and servants.

Given the community-oriented nature of our family structures, Indian women are swamped by the never-ending demands of caring for not only the home, husband and children but also for the aged. In the absence of an appropriate infrastructure, these can create intolerable pressures on the woman, especially if she also has a profession besides that of home-maker. Yet, the problems of women encumbered with these pressures have not figured on the agenda of any women's movement.

These pressures operate globally as well. Workplace norms make no allowances for the changed scenario. They have been framed for men who entered the public world unencumbered by demands of domesticity, child-rearing and housework. They do not entertain the double-sphere syndrome which most women face, and insist that women adapt to the all-male order or pay the price. Surprisingly, women themselves have not resisted this unreasonable demand. They have instead fallen over themselves to become what Friedan terms superwomen (*The Second Stage*, p. 56). They have even joined the male force in decrying those women who failed to pass the test.

In the Indian set-up, the lack of facilities like child-care and trained nurses can produce a no-exit situation for many women. It is interesting to note that while there have been attempts to modify the policy towards women at an official level, no effort has been made, except in the recently formulated 'Policy for Women' (Government of Maharashtra, June 1994), to prioritize issues like flexihours. Women who have had the courage to insist on these privileges have faced innumerable obstacles. They are black-listed for not being professional enough. In at least one case, a woman academic I know discovered that the story making the rounds at work was that she rushed home after her lectures because her daughter was 'abnormal' and dangerous if left alone.

The new 'Policy for Women' formulated by the Maharashtra government pin-points some of the anomalies between constitutional rights and social practice. It focuses on the role played by the government in minimizing the benefits admissible to Indian women under the constitution: 'The approach towards women was coloured by the "welfare" orientation where women were seen as an object of State munificence rather than as participants in the development process' (2.2, p. 3). It acknowledges that little has been done to 'attune Government thinking and Government machinery to the different but equally valid and relevant needs of women. The concepts of the "Man" and the "Public" domain; the "Woman" and the "Private" domain still continue to dominate Government thinking and therefore training programmes and plan schemes still do not clearly tackle the issues of infrastructure, support services and specific training which are so essential for women's development' (2.4, p.3).

Besides initiating the new policy, Maharashtra's former Chief Minister (1994), Sharad Pawar, has been one of the few men in government to publicly decry the persistent oppression of Indian women through the glorification of stultifying traditions and mythological stereotypes. However, it is doubtful whether one individual, however well-intentioned, can effect drastic changes. The universal conviction that men are inherently 'superior' and naturally dominate all gender-relations is far too rooted to give way easily without a fundamental change in consciousness among those who would implement the policy. Similarly, strategies like 'reservation' of employment for women would only devalue them further and could in fact *prevent* any real effort on the part of both women and men to correct existing injustices.

There is also the danger that policies like reservation could degenerate into forms of tokenism and distort the larger picture. Thus, the presence of large numbers of women in government, the administrative/bureaucratic machinery, or in universities may suggest that the Indian woman has never had it so good. The fallacy in such a conclusion has a lot to do with the fact that in terms of numbers alone, these women would constitute an infinitesimal minority. Moreover, they themselves are often caught in the dilemma of conservatism at a personal level. Finally, symbols can never be a satisfactory representation of the complex reality of women's lives.

This perception alone can rectify the sort of blinkered journalism that projects individual success stories as evidence of sweeping changes in the sociocultural milieu. Popular magazines in India are particularly susceptible to this disease and, in Chapter 1, I have referred to some to these stories. In an essay entitled 'The Unhappy Marriage of Marxism and Feminism: Can It Be Saved?', Carol Ehrlich warns that feminism is *not* about dressing for success, or measuring success in terms of one's position as a top executive or an elected official. Nor is it about having a wonderful marriage in which you and your husband have successful careers or go on marvellous vacations, or the time you spend with your lovely children because domestic help makes this possible. Ehrlich emphasizes that feminism has nothing to do, in particular, with things like 'becoming a police detective or CIA agent or marine corps general' (quoted by bell hooks in *Feminist theory: from margin to center,* South End Press, 1984, p. 7).

This warning is primarily about the relationship of feminism as an ideology to the values of Western society. These have been overwhelmingly in favour of the individual rather than the collective social good. Feminists like Zillah Eisenstein (*The Radical future of Liberal Feminism*, Longman, New York and London, 1981) and bell hooks (*margin* . . .) have discussed the limiting aspects of such values on the lives of the vast majority of women. hooks cautions us against assuming that merely seizing power in the existing social structure will ensure that we are nearer to ending female oppression: while this would give some women greater opportunities and more choices, and would therefore be an important advancement, it would not put an end to 'male domination as a system' (hooks, *margin* . . . , p. 90).

In the Indian context, however, patriarchal domination operates in another value context. The ethics of our society has always placed the community above the individual. This is as true for individual men as it is for the women. There have been other defining characteristics, such as caste, which have reinforced the patriarchal hierarchy and the constraints it places on individual freedom. It is worth noting that in both the Western and the Indian contexts, some of the earliest struggles against forms of patriarchal oppression had to do with religious domination. Women like Jaṇābāī and Kānhopātrā (Maharashtra, died around 1468) addressed their protests to God, and questioned the Hindu view of a human being's location in the hierarchy as inflexible. As already noted in Chapter 1, Jaṇābāī was clear that it was the smṛtis and their exponents who had reduced her, a woman and a śūdra to this condition. Kānhopātrā, a prostitute's daughter, upbraids God for his insensitivity:

While I call myself yours,
others enjoy my body:

tell me, who bears
the blame for this?

Even earlier, texts like Yāska's *Nirukta*, which predate the development of the patriarchal codes of the smṛtis, contain evidence of systems of thoughts wherein women enjoyed a rare degree of equality and social status. Though these have been blotted out of the popular consciousness by the patriarchal legacy of the dharmaśāstras, they are crucial evidence of an alternative system which could prove useful in the evolution of a feminist ethic shared by both men and women.

There have been innumerable scientific studies which have tried to explore the hierarchy of genetic evolution. Some of these have sparked off controversies, the most notorious one being the 1980s storm over the African 'Eve' who lived 200,000 years ago and, it was claimed, was the mother of us all. The fact remains that while paleoanthropologists squabble over their finds, and feminists mistakenly gloat over such early evidence of female legacy, the current debate about the status of women continues to assume bizarre dimensions.

Thus, over the last twenty years, in India, the evidence of the most gross forms of violence against women continues unabated. Mathura, a fourteen-year-old tribal girl from Maharashtra was raped by two policemen who were acquitted by the Supreme Court even though the Bombay High Court had convicted them. Maya Tyagi, travelling with her husband and his friends, was molested by two plainclothes policemen who later killed her husband, and paraded her naked through the town of Baghpat in Uttar Pradesh before taking her to the police station where she was raped.

These incidents took place in the late Seventies and early Eighties. In May 1993, Usha Dhiman of Saharanpur (also in Uttar Pradesh), who was falsely accused of theft, was dragged away from the court where she had come to surrender on the advice of her counsel who described what transpired when someone recognized her. She was dragged out of court by about fifteen or twenty people, stripped, mauled, and forcibly taken in the direction of the local police-station. The skin on her heels was torn off, and she was also bleeding (*The Indian Express, Sunday Magazine*, 18 July 1993). Though the police were not directly responsible for the attack on this occasion, their complicity with the mob who did this was clear.

The cases of bride-burning and dowry-related crimes, of girls being sexually exploited by Municipal Councillors and even Members of Legislative Assemblies (as in the Jalgaon sex-scandal,[1] and the Uttar Pradesh gang-rape of a Harijan girl, both of 1994), all in turn add up to an explosive scenario whose feudal core is aggravated by popular cinema with its increasing shift from the old love-lyrics to songs which brazenly assert a woman's commodity-status: '*Tu cheez badi hai mast, mast* . . .'[2] has surpassed even the crude suggestivity of the earlier '*Choli ke peeche kya hai*?'[3]

Western feminism had attacked pornography because of its essential exploitation of 'women's sexual and economic inequality for gain' (Catherine Mac-Kinnon, quoted by Fox-Genovese in *Feminism Without Illusions*, p. 91). They had argued that pornography was not a moral issue but one of sexual hierarchy and oppression (Fox-Genovese, p. 91). Gloria Steinem had described pornography as nothing less than 'sexual fascism' ('Erotica versus Pornography', in *Outrageous Acts and Everyday Rebellions,* p. 227).

The fact remains that in this, as in other areas, Western feminism has valuable lessons to offer. It is important that the shared concerned of women globally be recognized, along with the growth of divergent ideologies that have attempted to address them. At the same time it is necessary not to import them wholesale into the Indian context but to seek ways in which they could be indigenized. In going backwards to find out to what extent my experience of the present status of Indian women is contained in the past, this is what I have tried partially to understand.

This study makes no claim to be comprehensive. Its selectiveness is coloured by the attempt to see how the personal has a rationale in the politics of tradition. This politics has a tremendous mass appeal, and is blindly accepted by people who have failed to recognize that the sources of tradition need to be constantly subjected to rational scrutiny. If this book provokes Indian men and women to reassess dogmas they have taken for granted, it will have served its purpose even if the process proves some of my arguments wrong.

Notes

Chapter 1 : Our Women, Their Women

1. See Rajeswari Sunder Rajan, *Real and Imagined Women: gender, culture and postcolonialism,* Routledge, 1993, pp. 103–28, for a detailed analysis of 'the "case" of Indira Gandhi'.
2. Manjushree Sarda was murdered by her husband, Sharad Sarda, in Pune in 1982. Sharad Sarda was acquitted by the lower court, sentenced to death by the High Court, but given a reprieve by the Supreme Court 'on a vague theory of women's psychotic disorders' (Gandhi and Shah, p. 56).
3. Tarvinder Kaur was burnt to death on 17 May 1979 because she rebelled against the constant demands for money from her husband's family. Though she had clearly implicated her mother-in-law and sister-in-law in her dying statement, the police put her death down to suicide. This deliberate distortion of facts provoked angry protests and demonstrations by a group of women who mobilized themselves under the banner of the Stree Sangharsh (Women's Struggle). This campaign was one of the first organized protests against dowry murders.
4. Shahbano was married to Mohamad Ahmed Khan at the age of sixteen. After being married for forty-three years,

Shahbano found herself thrown out (1975) to be replaced by another wife. Her attempts to secure justice took a labyrinthine journey through the various Courts of the land and eventually resulted in the passing of the questionable and regressive Muslim Women's (Protection of Rights on Divorce) Act in 1986.

5. Roop Kanwar shot into the limelight in 1987, when she chose (or was made to choose) to become a sati. In spite of the media publicity, the State machinery could not (or did not) prevent the chunri mahotsav (a ceremony which honours a woman who has attained sati-hood), which became a mammoth public spectacle. Roop Kanwar has already become a legend.
6. Jaṇābāī died in 1350. Born a Śūdra, she worked as a maidservant in the house of the Marathi saint-poet Namdeo. Jaṇābāī overcame the constraints of gender and caste to become one of Maharashtra's leading saint-poets.
7. Mirābāī (AD 1498–1573), was married to Rāṇa Pratapsingh of the princely family of Jaipur. She gave up worldly comforts and immersed herself in total worship of Kṛṣṇa. Her verses have an unrestrained, almost sensual flavour.
8. Bahiṇābāī (AD 1628–1700) writes in a frank, straightforward, somewhat ironic style about faith and her own experiences as woman and disciple.
9. Bhāratīya nārī: the Indian woman, seen as prototype.
10. Sītā: wife of Rāma, protagonist of the *Rāmāyaṇa*, and believed to be an avatar of Viṣṇu.
11. Savitrī: Married to Satyavāna, she refuses to give him up to Yama, God of Death, and ultimately prevails with him.
12. Draupadī: Wife of the five Pāṇḍava brothers in the *Mahābhārata*. The reservations I mention may have something to do with this fact! Sītā and Sāvitrī are both ideal wives, who seek fulfilment through selfless service of their husbands. Draupadī is rather more independent and is shown as having very forceful views. All three

women are regarded as valid symbols of Indian womanhood even today, and have an enormous hold on the popular and creative consciousness.

13. Rambha: An apsara. (Used colloquially in Marathi to describe a woman of somewhat dubious attractions).
14. Hanumān, Sanjivanī: Hanumān, the son of Vāyu (wind) and leader of the monkeys, who became Rāma's most devoted follower. When Lakṣmaṇa was fatally wounded in the battle against Rāvaṇa in Lankā, Hanumān went in search of the Sanjivanī plant which is reputed to possess miraculous qualities and can revive a dead man. Unable to recognize the plant, Hanumān flew back to Lankā carrying the entire mountain on which it was said to grow.
15, Purush-jāti, strī-jāti: Jāti means class, nature, caste.
16. Purush and Strī signify male and female respectively. The two terms, therefore, encompass the two genders, imposing a casteist hierarchy as it were on the sexual one.
17. Strī-dharma: The code of conduct for a woman amounts in the orthodox Hindu world-view to a kind of faith. The phrase has not lost its meaning or relevance in contemporary Indian society.
18. Brahmachāryāsrama was the first stage, when the young boy was apprenticed to a guru. The second stage was when he married and became a 'householder'. In the third and fourth stages a man withdrew from the material world, first into the forest (vana), and then by renouncing the world altogether (sanyās).
19. Sowbhāgyavati: a married and unwidowed woman; by extension, therefore, a woman who dies before her husband; a woman, therefore, who is (literally) blessed with good fortune!
20. Ardhāngini: a woman who has merged her identity with her husband's. (Ardha-half; ang-body, being).
21. Haveli: the women's quarters in orthodox homes.
22. Chudiyaan, mangal-sūtra, kum-kum, sindoor, the colour

red, are all symbols of marriage which are doubly discriminatory. They are part of the traditional wife's attire, but they can only be worn as long as her husband is alive.

Chapter 2 : Gaurī-Kanyakā-Kumarī

1. *Daan do, tumhe beta ho jaayega*: 'If you give alms, you shall have a son.'
2. *Beti ho jaayegi*: 'You shall have a daughter.'
3. *Taittirīya Saṁhitā*: Saṁhitā refers to a collection of mantras (approximately 4000–1000 BC). The *Taittirīya Saṁhitā* is a mixture of prose and metrical mantras, and derives its name from the Tittira bird, which is black and white. This Saṁhitā is found in the Black Yajurveda (*Yajurveda*, the second of the four Vedas, is divided into the Black and White Yajurvedas).
4. Aitareya Brāhmaṇa: Brāhmaṇa means a ritual text. The Aitareya Brāhmaṇa is the ritual text of the *ṚgVeda* (the first of the four Vedas).
5. *Mahābhārata,* Ādiparvan: The Ādiparvan section of the Mahābhārata.
6. Bāṇa: Court-poet of King Harshavardhana.
7. Prabhākaravardhana: King Harshavardhana's father.
8. *Rubaab*: false notions about oneself; seeming over-smart.
9. Lakshmibai Tilak: (1873–1936). She was married to poet N.V. Tilak who became a Christian. Some time later, Lakshmibai herself was also converted to Christianity. Uneducated, she wrote an autobiography, *Smṛti-Chitre* (Vignettes from Memory) which has become something of a classic. She is regarded as being the first among modern Marathi poets.
10. Manu: Literally means 'the wise one'. Manu is also the name of a king who is believed to be the mythological ancestor of humankind. This is interesting in view of the fact that the *Manusmṛti* has acquired the status of a

sacred text. Though attributed to Manu, the text is believed to be the work of several Brahminical commentators.

11. *Manusmṛti*: A comprehensive treatise (200 BC–AD 200) covering all imaginable aspects relating to the life of a Hindu. My repeated references to this text are because I perceive it as central among all other similar texts, in terms of its hold over the popular consciousness.
12. Indira Sant: Born in 1914. Writes in a lyrical mode which also incorporates disturbing currents of female anguish, frustration and love. She writes of nature and of the contemporary woman's problems with equal involvement. She was the principal of a teacher's training college in Belgaum, Karnataka.
13. *Viṣṇupurāṇa*: One of the eighteen Mahapurāṇas (AD 600).
14. Anuśāsana: A parvan of the *Mahābhārata*.
15. *Mānava gr.*: Mānava Gṛhya-Sūtra. During the Vedic period, the Saṁhitās, Brāhmaṇas, Āraṇyakas and Upaniṣads were composed. The end of this period is referred to as the Sūtra period when the six *angas* of the Vedas (auxiliary texts to the Vedas) were composed. One of these was the Kalpa-Sūtra, which was concerned with Śrauta (Big Sacrifices), Gṛhya (domestic rituals) and Dharma (rules of general behaviour). The Mānava Gṛhya-Sūtra belongs to the second branch of the Kalpa-Sūtra.
16. Gautama: Law-giver, whose teachings are found in the Dharmasūtra of Gautama (approximately 600–300 BC).
17. Soma: God of intoxicants.
18. Gandharva: Celestial patron of music and dance.
19. Agni: God of fire.
20. Pitṛs: ancestors.
21. Parāśara: A law-giver, writer of the *Parāśara-Smṛti*.
22. Premchand: Twentieth century Hindi writer. Much of his fiction deals with social oppression and injustice.
23. *Āśv. gr.*: Āśvalāyana-gṛhya-sūtra. One of the

gṛhya-sūtras, going back to approximately 800–400 BC.
24. *Āp. gr.*: Āpastamba-gṛhya-sūtra. See note 23.
25. Kātyāyana: Law-giver. The Kātyāyanasmṛti, believed to date back to AD 400–600, has not yet been found.
26. Gotra: Originally meaning 'cow-stable' or 'herd of cows', it eventually came (in later Vedic times) to denote all those who were the descendants of a common male ancestor. According to Panini, there were eight primary gotras. 'The general conception about gotra is that it denotes all persons who trace descent in an unbroken male line from a common male ancestor' (Kane, *History of Dharmaśāstra,* Vol. II, p. 438).
27. *Śat. Br.*: Śatapatha Brāhmaṇa. Brāhmaṇa text of the Vājasaneyī Saṁhitā of the White Yajurveda.
28. *Vadhū-parīkṣā*: Literally, the testing of the bride. Some of these tests are listed in this chapter. Today, before a marriage is arranged, it is common for the bridegroom's party to scrutinize her thoroughly before giving their approval.
29. *Kāma-Sūtra*: composed by Vātsyāyana (AD third century).
30. *Bhātuklīs*: playing at keeping house. A popular girls' pastime in the Maharashtra of my girlhood, it involves getting together and cooking/preparing various dishes.

Chapter 3 : Vivāha

1. Saṁskāras: ceremonial or transformative rituals.
2. Kane, *History of Dharmaśāstra*, Vol. II, Part 1, p.427.
3. Rāvaṇa: king of Lankā, and abductor of Sītā.
4. Lakṣmaṇa-rekhā: a line Lakṣmaṇa is supposed to have drawn before he left Sītā alone. Sītā was told not to cross the line under any circumstance.
5. Padma Gole: Born in 1913. A Marathi poet who questions conventional gender-attitudes in her work.
6. Mathura, a fourteen-year-old tribal girl from Maharashtra, had been raped by two police constables

who were acquitted by the Supreme Court. The judges who reversed the verdict of the Bombay High Court held that the alleged 'rape' was actually a willing act, and that Mathura had had sex with the two policemen who were strangers to her. According to the judges, Mathura was of dubious moral character: she was not a virgin and had a boyfriend in spite of her family's objections! Further, the policemen showed no physical injuries, which meant she could not have fought them. Ergo, the accusation of rape was a defamatory falsehood.

7. *Izzat*: honour, self-respect, reputation.
8. Swayaṁvar: a ceremony at which the bride, usually a princess, chose her own groom from among an assembly of kings and princes gathered there for the purpose. Sometimes, the bride's hand was won in a contest of strength/skill etc.
9. Hira Bansode: Born in 1939. She was married at fourteen, but managed to pursue her studies and get a post-graduate degree. While her poetry speaks of gender-injustice as a whole, much of it also deals with the double injustice experienced by a woman who belongs to a low caste.
10. Ahilya: a woman who was seduced by the god Indra who disguised himself as her husband. It is said that Ahilya slept with Indra even though she saw through his disguise. Because of this, her husband, Gautama-munī, cursed her, transforming her to stone. She was eventually liberated by the touch of Rāma's foot.
11. Kāli: consort of Śiva, in her avengeful form.
12. Bhiṣma: The patriarch in the *Mahābhārata*. Said to be the eighth son of the river goddess Ganga. Ganga is supposed to have killed the first seven as soon as they were born. The eighth, Bhiṣma, was saved because of the desperate pleading of King Śāntanu, who was Ganga's mortal husband.
13. Yudhiṣṭhira: eldest of the Pāṇḍavas, the five sons of Pāṇḍu to whom Draupadī was married.

14. When Draupadī was about to be stripped naked, she asked the assembly and, in particular, Bhiṣma, whether Yudhiṣṭhira who had already gambled away his freedom had the right to stake her. Bhiṣma replied that the law was too complex for him to be able to answer her satisfactorily, but that '[Though it is true that] a person in not entitled to stake anything that does not belong to him, [still, it is also true that] a woman belongs to her husband [in whatever circumstances he might be placed].' Sharad Patil, who quotes this passage from the *Mahābhārata*, II.67.47, has the following observations to make: 'Bhiṣma declared in unmistakable terms that though Yudhiṣṭhira had already gambled away his freedom to the Kauravas, he had not lost his ownership of Draupadī, and hence even as a "slave" he was "master" enough to dispose of the freedom of his wife. Draupadī, his grand daughter-in-law, or a wife in general, was according to Bhiṣma, a slave's slave!' (*Dāsa-Śūdra Slavery,* p.157).
15. Sabhāparva: One of the parvans of the *Mahābhārata.*
16. The two were commonly equated. D.D. Kosambi quotes from the Gita (9.32) the following lines (attributed to Kṛṣṇa himself), to support his claim that the Gita was sung for the upper classes by the Brahmins, and only through them for others: 'For those who take refuge in Me, be they even of the *sinful breeds such as women, vaiśyas and śūdras*' (*Myth and Reality: Studies in the Formation of Indian Culture,* Popular Prakashan, Bombay, 1962, p.15).
17. Jayarāma: Jayarāma Gosāvī, a Brahmin ascetic through whose kīrtans Bahīnabāī was led to Tukaram.
18. Pāṇḍurang: another name for Vitthal (Viṣṇu).
19. Gāyatrī mantra: composed by Viśvāmitra (the third mandala of the *Ṛg Veda*).

Chapter 4 : Vaidhavya

1. *Skandapurāṇa*: One of the Mahapurāṇas (AD 300–600).
2. *Yājñavalkya-smṛti*: AD 100–300.
3. Bṛhaspati: one of the law-givers, author of the *Bṛhaspatismṛti* (AD 300–500) which has not yet been found.
4. Bahiṇābāī Choudhari: Born in Maharashtra in 1880, died in 1951. Not the Bahiṇābāī referred to earlier. She came from an uneducated farming family in Khandesh, and much of her poetry was composed while working in the fields and around the house.

Chapter 6 : Wife and Mother

1. Nārada: The Nāradasmṛti, AD 100–400.
2. Married to the blind Dhṛtarāṣṭra, Gāndharī chose to spend the rest of *her* life blind-folded.
3. *Viṣnu Dharma Sūtra*: AD 100–300.
4. 'Vanaparava': the Vanaparvan of the *Mahābhārata*.
5. Enlightenment: Roughly the period of the new rationalism (AD 1650–1800) in the West.
6. Sanskṛti: culture.
7. Śankha-Likhita: this assertion is quoted in *Smṛticandrikā*, AD 1200–1225.

Chapter 7 : Postscript

1. A murky scandal involving young girls who were filmed in compromising positions and then blackmailed. A somewhat unusual real-life version of sex, lies, and video-tapes!
2. 'You are a super, super piece of goods.'
3. 'What's behind the choli?'

Bibliography

Campbell, Joseph (ed.): *Myths and Symbols in Indian Art and Civilization* (Pantheon Books, Bollingen Series VI, 4th printing, 1963, p.139)

Chaudhuri, Nirad C. : *Hinduism* (OUP, 1979)

Cott, Nancy F. : *The Grounding of Modern Feminism* (Yale University Press, New Haven and London, 1987)

Davis, Elizabeth Gould: *The First Sex* (Penguin, 1978)

de Beauvior, Simone: *The Second Sex* (Penguin, 1977)

Doniger, Wendy and Brian K. Smith (tr.): *The Laws of Manu* (Penguin India, 1992)

Eisenstein, Zillah R. : *The Radical Future of Liberal Feminism* (Longman, New York and London, 1981)

Evans, Sara M.: *Born for Liberty* (The Free Press, New York, Collier Macmillan Publishers, London, 1989)

Faludi, Susan: *Backlash: The Undeclared War Against American Women* (Crown Publishers, New York, 1991)

Fox-Genovese, Elizabeth: *Feminism Without Illusions: A Critique of Individualism* (University of North Carolina Press, Chapel Hill and London, 1991)

Friedan, Betty: *The Feminine Mystique* (WW Norton and Company Inc., New York, 1963)

——. *The Second Stage* (Summit Books, New York, 1981)

Gandhi, Nandita and Nandita Shah: *The Issues at Stake:*

Theory and Practice in the Contemporary Women's Movement in India (Kali for Women, New Delhi, 1991)

Ghadially, Rehana (ed.): *Women in Indian Society; A Reader* (Sage Publications, New Delhi, 1988)

Giffon, Frederick C.: *Woman as Revolutionary* (Mentor, 1973)

Greer, Germaine: *The Female Eunuch* (Bantam Books, 1972)

hooks, bell: *Ain't I A Woman: Black Women and Feminism* (South End Press, 1981)

——. *Feminist Theory: from margin to center* (South End Press, 1984)

Joseph, Ammu and Kalpana Sharma: *Whose News? The Media and Women's Issues* (Sage Publications, New Delhi, 1994)

Jung, Anees: *Unveiling India: A Woman's Journey* (Penguin India, 1987)

Kane, P.V. :*History of Dharmaśāstra* (Bhandarkar Oriental Research Institute, Poona, 1941)

Kosambi, D.D.: *Myth and Reality: Studies in the Formation of Indian Culture* (Popular Prakashan, Bombay, 1962)

Millett, Kate: *Sexual Politics* (Doubleday and Company Inc., New York, 1970)

Minai, Naila: *Women in Islam: Tradition and Transition in the Middle East* (Seaview Books, New York, 1981)

Morgan, Robin (ed.): *Sisterhood is Powerful: An Anthology of Writings from the Women's Liberation Movement* (Random House, New York, 1970)

——. *The Word of a Woman: Feminist Dispatches 1968-1992* (WW Norton and Company Inc., New York, 1992)

Papanek, Hanna and Gail Minault: *Separate Worlds: Studies of Purdah in South Asia* (Chanakya Publications, New Delhi, 1982)

Patil, Sharad: *Dāsa-Śūdra Slavery: Studies in the Origin of Indian Slavery and Feudalism and their Philosophies* (Allied Publishers, New Delhi, 1982)

Rajan, Rajeswari Sunder : *Real and Imagined Women:*

gender, culture and postcolonialism (Routledge, New York and London, 1993)
Rich, Adrienne : *Of Woman Born: Motherhood as Experience and Institution* (WW Norton and Company Inc., New York, 1976)
Rohini P.H., S.V. Sujata and C. Neelam (eds.) : *'My Life is One Long Struggle' : Women, Work, Organisation and Struggle* (Pratishabd, Belgaum)
Rowbotham, Sheila : *Woman's Consciousness, Man's World* (Pelican, 1973)
——. *The Past is Before Us* (Beacon Press, 1989)
Sangari, Kumkum and Sudesh Vaid: *Recasting Women: Essays in Colonial History* (Kali for Women, New Delhi, 1991)
Sathe, S.P.: *Towards Gender Justice* (Research Centre for Women's Studies, SNDT Women's University, Bombay, 1993)
Sen, Ilina (ed.): *A Space Within the Struggle: Women's Participation in People's Movements* (Kali for Women, New Delhi, 1990)
Spivak, Gayatri Chakravorty: *In Other Worlds: Essays in Cultural Politics* (Routledge, New York and London, 1988)
Spong, John Shelby: *Born of a Woman: A Bishop Rethinks the Birth of Jesus* (Harper, San Francisco, 1992)
Steinem, Gloria: *Outrageous Acts and Everyday Rebellions* (Holt, Rinehart and Winston, New York, 1983)
Young, Serinity (ed.): *Anthology of Sacred Texts By and About Women* (New York, Pandora, Harper Collins, 1993)

Index

READ MORE IN PENGUIN